Praise for the Next Story

The digital revolution is one of the most important developments of our times. Christians need good, solid, and insightful guidance as to how to engage the digital world without surrendering to the digital mind. Tim Challies is uniquely qualified to write this book, and I greet its arrival with enthusiasm.

Dr. R. Albert Mohler Jr., president, The
Southern Baptist Theological Seminary

There are many books evaluating the nature and impact of new media. There are many books on Christian discipleship. However, this book brings these issues together, with profound simplicity and well-informed analysis. This is an important book not only for church leaders but for all who seek to understand how we are used by our technology as well as use it.

Michael Horton, professor at Westminster
Seminary and cohost of The White Horse Inn

Tim Challies knows technology, and he knows the faith. So when he writes on the intersection of technology and faith, it is a must-read. *The Next Story* gives solid counsel to living out the gospel in the context of today's rapid progression of technology.

Ed Stetzer, www.edstetzer.com

All of us today—whether digital immigrants or digital natives—are living in the aftershock of the digital explosion. Though our world has radically changed, the fundamental question remains the same: Will we be found faithful? Tim Challies proves to be a faithful navigator, though humble enough to admit that he identifies with the rest of us as a fellow struggler. The result of his labors is an accessible guide full of wise reflection and practical counsel. What hath technology to do with the biblical worldview? Come and see.

Justin Taylor, blogger ("Between Two Worlds")
and managing editor of the ESV Study Bible

No one I know is more thoughtfully connected to and wisely critical of the digital universe that envelops us than Tim Challies. In *The Next Story*, he helps us navigate the rapidly expanding digital explosion. The beauty of the book is not simply its wow factor ("I had no idea all of that was happening on the web …"), but more importantly its heart concern ("How do I stay virtuous in a virtual world?"). Challies's work is cutting-edge in the best sense, helping Christians to sever themselves from the sin that so easily (and subtly) entangles in order to run the race that glorifies Christ.

Bryan Chapell, president of
Covenant Theological Seminary

We all marvel at the rapid technological advances that have taken place in our lifetime. But few of us stop to reflect on the profound way these changes are shaping what it means to be human. *The Next Story* is a great place to start. It moves beyond warnings simply to be careful about what we see (important though this is) to calls to explore how new technology affects how we know God, relate to other people, and even think. Instead of giving simplistic rules or proof texts, it offers a penetrating analysis of the modern world in light of the biblical story, along with practical principles about how technology can be your tool and not your master.

Tim Chester, leader in The Crowded House, an
international family of church plants

As the coauthor of thirteen words in Tim's new book, I'm happy that he, with his skill as a writer, his experience as a web designer, and his deeply informed, discerning faith, wrote the other 75,000. Tim's new book helps believers better understand and live faithfully in the electronic age. Rather than blindly embracing or fearfully rejecting new media and technology, Tim skillfully weaves together biblical wisdom, historical background, and critical insight, giving readers practical application they can use today.

John Dyer, director of web development at Dallas
Theological Seminary

As someone who has spent almost two decades helping couples and families grow stronger and thrive, I have seen how the digital explosion is sending shock waves through homes—everything from Facebook-threatened marriages to couples who can't have a conversation that goes deeper than a tweet. It is time we think seriously about the subtle ways in which technology is reordering our lives. In *The Next Story*, Tim Challies helps us do that.

Bob Lepine, cohost of FamilyLife Today

If I outsource memory, is it an advance or a loss? Where is wisdom in the immediacy of the information explosion? Can we really affirm biblical authority when Wikipedia is truth? Tim Challies uses theoretical, experiential, and theological lenses to give a prophetic assessment of our digital age. He unpacks the opportunities of increased connection as well as the new Gnosticism of the dis-incarnations of the virtual society. He calls us to extricate ourselves from the ADHD world of information overload to live as whole persons who give ourselves to wisdom and worship of God alone.

Gerry Breshears, PhD, professor of systematic theology
at Western Seminary

When we think about technology, most of us are content to focus naively on features and price. Thankfully, Tim Challies calls us to something deeper. *The Next Story* is a compelling call for God's people to consider technology's implications, effects, and tendencies. Challies demonstrates thoughtful examination of what technology can do to us rather than just what it can do for us.

Scott McClellan, Echo Conference, exploring the
intersection of media, technology, and the church

TIM CHALLIES

THE

LIFE AND FAITH AFTER

NEXT

THE DIGITAL EXPLOSION

STORY

ZONDERVAN®

ZONDERVAN.com/
AUTHORTRACKER
follow your favorite authors

ZONDERVAN

The Next Story
Copyright © 2011 by Tim Challies

This title is also available as a Zondervan ebook. Visit www.zondervan.com/ebooks.

This title is also available in a Zondervan audio edition. Visit www.zondervan.fm.

Requests for information should be addressed to:

Zondervan, *Grand Rapids, Michigan 49530*

ISBN 978-0-310-32903-9

Published in association with the literary agency of Wolgemuth & Associates, Inc.

Cover design: Micah Kandros
Interior design: Kirk Luttrell & Ben Fetterley

Printed in the United States of America

11 12 13 14 15 16 /DCI/ 23 22 21 20 19 18 17 16 15 14 13 12 11 10 9 8 7 6 5 4 3 2 1

For my brothers Pat, Andrew, Rick, and Justin—
one by birth, three by marriage, all four in the Lord.

Contents

Part 1

The Mandate of Technology
The Morality of Technology
The Heart and Technology

Technology Involves Both Risk and Opportunity
The Medium Is the Message
Technology Is Ecological
Technology Shifts Power
Technology Is Biological

Digital Prehistory
The Information Age
The Rise of the Image
The Dawn of the Digital
The Conquest of the Digital

Part 2

The Growth of Communication
The Challenges of Communication
Speaking, Truthing, Loving
To Whom Much Is Given . . .
Application :: Christian Communication
Questions for Reflection

What Is Media?
Face-to-Face
Digital Disincarnation
Real Space and Cyberspace

Preface

On October 30, 1961, the Soviet Union detonated the most powerful weapon ever created. Nicknamed Tsar Bomba, the king of bombs, it was a multistage thermonuclear warhead with explosive power in the range of 50 megatons — equivalent to detonating 50 million tons of TNT. This made it fourteen hundred times more powerful than the *combined* force of the nuclear bombs that the United States dropped on Hiroshima and Nagasaki in the closing days of the Second World War. In fact, the explosive force of this bomb alone was ten times greater than the total amount of explosives deployed in the entire war, *including* those two nuclear bombs.

It is hard for most of us to understand what 50 million tons of TNT would look like, so let's try this: Imagine that you had an Olympic-sized swimming pool full of it, packed from end to end, from top to bottom. Try to imagine the devastation you would bring about in igniting that quantity of one of the most powerful explosives in the world. What if you had ten of those pools full of it? Or a hundred? Or a thousand? 50 million tons is the equivalent of filling 11,000 Olympic-sized swimming pools with TNT and igniting it all simultaneously. And in Tsar Bomba all of that destructive power was contained in a single bomb that was 26 feet long and 6 feet in diameter.

Truly this was a weapon of unparalleled destruction.*

At 11:32 a.m. the weapon detonated 13,000 feet above the surface of the Mityushikha Bay test range, on a Barents Sea island far above the Arctic Circle. The flash of light from the explosion was visible over 600 miles away, though it would take 49 minutes for the sound to reach that distance. The fireball reached from the ground to 34,000 feet in the air, and a person standing 60 miles away from the blast would have experienced third-degree burns from the heat. The mushroom cloud rose almost 40 miles into the sky, seven times higher than Mount Everest, and had a diameter of nearly 25 miles. Windows were shattered as far as 600 miles away. The shock wave, initially measuring 7.1 on the Richter Scale, was still measurable on its third passage around the circumference of the earth.

Some time after the detonation, a team was sent to ground zero, the epicenter of the explosion, to see the results. They reported, not surprisingly, that there had been utter devastation.[1] "The ground surface

---

*Thanks to Jeff Patterson, Chris Roth, and Tom Gee for figuring out the math for me. Yes, it took three of them (one to do the work and the other two to correct him).

of the island has been levelled, swept and licked so that it looks like a skating rink. The same goes for rocks. The snow has melted and their sides and edges are shiny. There is not a trace of unevenness in the ground.... Everything in this area has been swept clean, scoured, melted and blown away."[2] The area of total and complete destruction was fully 44 miles in diameter.

Mityushikha Bay had been blown apart, but it had also been blown together, combined in new ways. You see, Tsar Bomba was a thermonuclear weapon, a hydrogen bomb—one that used nuclear *fusion* to cause devastation exponentially greater than anything that had previously been detonated. On a chemical level, much had been destroyed—and much had been created. Out of the chaos of destruction a strange new order had emerged. Trees, plants, and animals had been blown to bits, reduced to their component parts. Hills had been leveled and valleys filled. What remained was a smooth and unnatural landscape both terrible and haunting. The rocks had not ceased to exist but had been reshaped, smoothed, and molded into new forms.

Mityushikha Bay was not gone; it was changed, altered forever.

Ten years after Tsar Bomba was detonated over Mityushikha Bay, another explosion occurred. Though it lacked the power and spectacle of Tsar Bomba, it has had a far greater impact on the world. In 1971, scientists at Intel Corporation introduced the Intel 4004, the world's first commercially available microprocessor. The 4004 was the first and most rudimentary of what would eventually become a long line of processors that would find their way into nearly everything we own. As they shrank in size and increased in power, microprocessors were integrated into calculators, computers, televisions, mobile phones, automobiles, and toys. The invention of the microprocessor was a spark igniting the explosive growth of digital technology. Like Tsar Bomba, this digital "explosion" has reshaped the landscape of our lives, destroying and creating, splitting things apart and bringing them together in new ways.

Over the past three decades, digital technologies have powerfully changed our lives. They are woven into the very way we understand and relate to the world around us. We are now a digital culture. We are no longer who and what we were just a few decades ago.

The
DIGITAL
EXPLOSION

The Digital Explosion

This book began with a question. Actually, it began with an uneasy feeling that begged a whole series of heartfelt questions. I live as a writer and a web editor, spending most of my life sitting before a screen surrounded by the latest and greatest high-tech devices. And I began to feel overwhelmed. I began to feel as if maybe, just maybe, all of my devices, gizmos, and gadgets owned me as much as I owned them. Even worse, I came to see that these devices were constantly demanding my time and attention. They buzzed and beeped and blinked and called me to respond to them. Worse still, they quickly grew obsolete, falling out of favor and leading me to want newer, upgraded models.

All of this made me uneasy. I began to wonder: Am I giving up control of my life? Is it possible that these technologies are changing me? Am I becoming a tool of the very tools that are supposed to serve me?

I went searching for people who were asking similar questions, men and women who have taken time to think about what it means to live in a *digital* world, a world surrounded by gadgets, a world in which we define and understand ourselves in completely new ways. I found that there were others who have been asking these questions—doctors, sociologists, theologians, technologists, philosophers. From some of them I learned *how* and *why* our gadgets have come to figure so prominently in our lives. Others provided helpful insight on how technology functions in human society. And from a precious few I began to learn how Christians can live in a digital world with virtue and dignity.

The digital revolution is global, reaching to the farthest corners of the earth. It affects the way we see, what we hear, how we interact with the world around us, and how we communicate with others. Swimming in this digital sea, we are caught up in a torrent of media, striving to stay afloat and make some headway against the rush of sounds, images, and words that seem intent on drowning us out. Some, like Rip Van Winkle, are just now waking up to this new reality. They rub their eyes and wonder what has happened. How has the world changed so quickly and so thoroughly? Others have been born into it—they are digital natives who have never known a world apart from digital technology.

As I read, reflected, and wrote, I found myself identifying with a little poem written by Danny Hillis, a technologist responsible for creating much of the computer architecture that lives within the machines we increasingly take for granted. Even Hillis, a computer genius and digital pioneer in his own right, knew that something profound had happened. He, too, wondered just how the digital explosion would reshape our cultural story—our understanding of ourselves and the world we live in.

> In some sense, we've
> run out of our story, which
> we were operating on, which
> was the story of power taking over nature—it's not
> that we've finished that, but
> we've gotten ahead of ourselves, and
> we don't know what
> the next story is after that.[1]

I asked myself, *Is Hillis right?* Have we "run out of our story"? And if so, what comes next? How has the digital explosion reshaped our understanding of ourselves, our world, and, most importantly, our knowledge of God? And what is "the next story" that will inform and direct the way we live?

The Bible reveals that we are created and called to fulfill God's mandate: that we go into all the world, faithfully stewarding the world God has created and the message he has given us. Thankfully, God has already provided a story for our lives. It is a story of subduing nature and caring for his creation. It is a story each of us has been born into and one in which we all have a part to play.

From the beginning, technology has played a vital role in this story, of course. God has gifted human beings with remarkable ability to dream, create, and invent technologies that serve us as we serve him, technologies that enable us to *better* serve him. But if technology is a good gift from God, with the potential to help us fulfill our God-given calling and purpose, why does it so often feel like we are slaves to our technology, like we are serving it instead of demanding that it serve us?

- We see a woman who walks away from her local church to become a member of a virtual church community tied together by little more than a website, and we wonder if virtual community can truly replace the physical presence of other believers.
- We sit in church and spot a young person using his mobile phone to send and receive text messages during worship, and we wonder whether he owns his phone—or it owns him.
- We see a family out for dinner and spot a dad talking on his phone while the kids play with their handheld gaming systems—every member of the family lost in his or her own little digital world—and we shake our heads and wonder, *What has gone wrong with the world?*
- We see young men immersing themselves in video games, content to spend endless hours staring at their screens, losing themselves in virtual worlds that must somehow seem so much more interesting and attractive than the real world.
- We see students dedicating vast amounts of time to social websites like Facebook, suspecting that amid all of this online socializing, they are missing out on the beauty of real-world, face-to-face friendships.

We wonder if maybe, just maybe, we *have* gotten ahead of ourselves a little bit. Maybe we *don't* know what we are doing. Maybe, just maybe, we have become slaves to our own devices. Maybe we haven't considered the consequences of the digital revolution, much less the way it is impacting our faith. How, then, are we to live?

We cannot run away from digital technology—mobile phones and computers and the Internet and television are likely to be with us in one form or another for some time. Nor would we necessarily want to run away from them. Certainly, not all technology is harmful or dangerous. Is there a way, then, to live virtuously, immersed in this strange new digital reality?

I'd like to invite you to join me as we think about the "next story," a story we are living right now—life after the digital explosion. We'll explore some suggestions and ideas for how we as Christians can live in this new reality with character, virtue, and wisdom. And we'll examine how we can respond to these revolutionary changes as followers of Christ in a digital age, learning to live faithfully as the next story unfolds.

Rich and Poor

Author Malcolm Gladwell generalizes that today we are experience rich and *theory* poor. And so he has taken to writing books, he says, to find new ways of making sense of the world and uncovering connections between things that would otherwise appear to be disconnected. Through his books he wants to say, "Here is where history meets culture or where culture meets history."[2]

To Gladwell's aphorism I might dare to add that we are also experience rich and *theology* poor. Each of us has had plenty of experience with technology, but few of us have the theoretical or theological tools to make sense of the consequences of our use of technology. And so we find a tension between how we *use* technology, how we *know* technology operates, and how *God* expects us to use technology.

Maybe we can best illustrate all of this with a diagram:

Here we have technology in theory, theology, and experience, but there is no overlap between them; each exists in its own separate sphere. Many of us live in the experience circle, where we have never invested any significant effort in understanding the theory of technology and have never paused to even consider the theological dimension of technology. We *use*

technology without thinking deeply about it, without really understanding what it is or how it impacts our lives and our hearts.

Perhaps you have read *Amusing Ourselves to Death* or *Technopoly* by Neil Postman or *The Medium is the Massage** by Marshall McLuhan. Or maybe you've had moments, as I have, when you've begun to think about the way technology operates in your life. If so, you've already begun to integrate the theoretical and the experiential. You aren't just blindly using technology; you are thinking about it, asking questions. Hopefully, if you were interested enough to pick up this book, you're already living in that overlap, the place where theory intersects experience so that the way you use technology is informed by what you know to be true about it. You are a "thoughtful" user of technology, unwilling to blindly accept it without critically considering the impact it will have on your life.

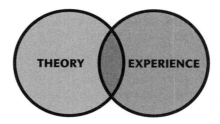

I've said that a "thoughtful" user of technology lives in that space where theory and experience intersect. Now, because we are interested in living in a *distinctly Christian* way, let's add another dimension: theology.

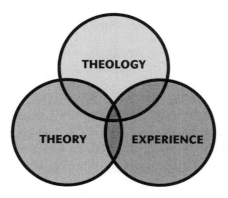

---

*No, this isn't a typo. The title of the book includes a typo in which an editor misspelled *message* as *massage*. McLuhan left the typo in place because he thought it helped prove his thesis.

What does theology have to do with technology? More than you might think! In fact, one of the aims of this book is to take us to that point in the middle, that point where all three circles converge. We are looking for that sweet spot where our use of technology is not just thoughtful and informed, but it is informed by the Bible, by an understanding of God's purpose for technology. In that place of thoughtful, technological discernment, we live in light of what we know to be true about technology, what we know to be true about ourselves, and what we know to be true about the God who made us.

There are many books we could choose to read on any one of these topics. Quite a few manage to draw two of the circles together. But as I have read and studied, I have found very few that have succeeded in focusing on the confluence of the three. As this book progresses, we will look at each of the circles, but our focus will be on living where the three converge. It does us no good to know how to use technology if we haven't critically questioned our use of it. And it does us no good to use technology, even with critical insight, if we don't understand the God-given reason and purpose for technology.

There are several different ways in which Christians can respond to the digital world. Some are tempted to embrace the latest technological discoveries enthusiastically and unthinkingly. They will argue that cell phones and video games and computers are an inevitable part of life in the twenty-first century. They will suggest that we must simply embrace these new technologies or the church will risk becoming irrelevant to a world shaped and influenced by digital technology. But such an unqualified embrace lacks appropriate discernment and is unwise. God calls us to use our minds, to use our Spirit-filled hearts, to distinguish between good and evil, between right and wrong, even in our use of technology.

If the first response is enthusiastic embrace, a second possibility for some Christians is strict separation, keeping themselves from these technologies and seeing everything digital as a dangerous enemy. Such persons will necessarily withdraw from the world and seek to keep themselves free from digital defilement. While there is something to commend in this approach, it is not at all realistic. Digital technologies are an unavoidable part of today's world and there is no biblical reason to utterly separate ourselves from them. As we will see, digital technology is not inherently evil. It can and must be used in ways that honor and glorify God.

The third response, and the response that most readers of this book will likely take, is that of the discerning Christian. While there is a range of possible responses—from enthusiastic embrace to strict separation—the response of the thinking Christian should be *disciplined discernment*. In this approach, a Christian looks carefully at the new realities, weighs and evaluates them, and educates himself, thinking deeply about the potential consequences and effects of using a particular technology. Through it all, even as he is using a specific technology, he disciplines himself to be discerning, to embrace what can be embraced and to reject what needs to be rejected. He moves beyond the broad strokes of utter rejection and complete acceptance. Instead, he relies on the Holy Spirit, who speaks his wisdom through the Bible, to learn how he can live with virtue in this new digital world.[3]

The Unfolding of the Next Story

In part 1 of this book, we will look to theology, theory, and experience. We will begin at the beginning, so to speak, as we see how God intended technology to function in the world he created. We will then turn to the theoretical, seeking to understand what is always true about the relationship between humans and their technologies. And finally we will pause to gain a historical perspective that will allow us to see how we came to live in this strange new digital world.

In part 2, we will look to areas of application specific to the Christian life, showing how we can live with wisdom and virtue in this digital world, using our technologies without being used by them:

- We will see that digital living offers particular challenges and opportunities for Christians.
- We will see that we now live a mediated reality, one in which some kind of media constantly stands between us and the rest of the world.
- We will see that we are increasingly distracted, pulled from one task to the next, from one media to the next.
- We will see that information is a compelling new kind of idol that calls us to invest our trust in it.
- We will see that we are now a hypersocial people and why we must intentionally submit our need for constant communication to the lordship of God.
- We will see that the digital explosion has resulted in significant changes in authority structures that affect us, our families, and our churches.
- We will see that this digital world brings with it entirely new conceptions of privacy and visibility.

Through it all we will let God's Word, the Bible, guide, inform, and convict us. It may seem counterintuitive that in our quest to seek how we can live with virtue in a digital age, we will rely on a book that is thousands of years old — a book that was first recorded not on a computer or even paper, but on old, dusty scrolls. Before that, it lived only in human memory, passed from one person to the next through oral transmission. Our first impulse may be to scoff at such a thing, wondering how we could possibly learn from those who thought bronze spears were a near-miraculous invention. Yet it is exactly the Bible's long track record that gives it credence on this topic. It has survived and thrived through every technological change and every technological era. The wisdom that has steered humans since the earliest days can surely direct us as well. And so we begin, trusting God to guide us, as we look at life and faith after the digital explosion.

PART 1

CHAPTER 1

DISCERNING TECHNOLOGY

My son has a rather odd habit when he talks on the telephone. When a friend calls him, he takes the phone and immediately begins to pace, walking in circles around the house. He starts in the kitchen, walks down the hall to the front door, turns left into the living room, walks through the dining room, and then heads back into the kitchen, completing a full circuit of our home. And as he talks, he paces, going around and around, again and again.

Recently, I was rather surprised to find myself doing the very same thing. Talking on the telephone with a friend, I noticed that I, too, was pacing around and around our house as I talked. You are probably familiar with the old expression "he's a chip off the old block." It's a phrase we use to describe a person who bears a resemblance to his father. It can be a physical resemblance, but more often than not, it's a similarity we notice in personality or habits. We see certain traits in a person and recognize that he shares something in common with his father. My son walks while he talks on the phone because I walk while I talk on the phone. Like father, like son.

In the first chapter of the Bible, we read that God created man in his own image. "Let us make man in our image, after our likeness," said God. "And let them have dominion over the fish of the sea and over the birds of the heavens and over the livestock and over all the earth and over every creeping thing that creeps on the earth" (Genesis 1:26). These words are so well-known to us that they have undoubtedly lost much of their power. They tell us that we have been made to resemble the Creator of the universe; we are, to put it lightly, "chips off the old block." God, the Creator of all that exists, saw fit to share with us many of his divine attributes. Like God, we, too, are spiritual beings. We are able to love. We have a kind of moral freedom.

And we are able to create.

Just as God created, we create. God has given human beings the ability to think, to come up with remarkable ideas, to be innovative. Technology is simply the practical result of the creative process. Birds may instinctually use spiderwebs to build nests. A monkey may somehow discover how to use a rock to crack open a nut. But these aren't creative activities leading to new technologies. Animals don't act out of a desire to do something unique or distinct. They simply respond to their hard-wired instincts and do what they were made to do. But human beings create because of a God-given ability to be creative. And the practical result of our creative activity is something we call *technology*.

Our creative abilities have led us to craft all sorts of different technologies, from the most basic to the most advanced. We dream; we imagine new possibilities; we think of creative solutions. And in all of these activities we resemble our Creator. Ultimately, then, God himself is the author of all technology.

The Mandate of Technology

If bearing the image of God is what gives us our *ability* to create, God's mandate—his commanded purpose for human beings—is what drives our *desire* to create. When God created man in his image, he did it with a purpose in mind. He created man to have dominion over the world that he had created, to act as his appointed representative to the creation. No sooner had God formed man than he assigned a job to him. "And God blessed them. And God said to them, 'Be fruitful and multiply and fill the earth and subdue it and have dominion over the fish of the sea and over the

birds of the heavens and over every living thing that moves on the earth' "
(Genesis 1:28). Man was to be fruitful and multiply, to fill the earth with
more people. And he was also to subdue the earth, to rule over it for God's
sake, to be a reflector of God's glory. Theologians sometimes call this God-
given purpose the *creation mandate*. Author Nancy Pearcey writes,

> In Genesis, God gives what we might call the first job description: "Be
> fruitful and multiply and fill the earth and subdue it." The first phrase,
> "be fruitful and multiply" means to develop the social world: build
> families, churches, schools, cities, governments, laws. The second phrase,
> "subdue the earth," means to harness the natural world: plant crops,
> build bridges, design computers, compose music.[1]

God's basic instruction to mankind is to develop the resources of the natural
world and use God-given abilities to bring glory to him. To put it in more
practical terms, God is glorified in our creativity, whether that leads us to
craft a painting that moves our hearts to praise or to design a plow that will
better allow us to plant and harvest a crop. To do these things — building
cities and schools and families, planting crops and composing music —
we must rely on the practical fruit of our creative abilities: technology.
Technology is *the creative activity of using tools to shape God's creation for
practical purposes.*[2]

God made us creative beings in his image and assigned to us a task that
would require us to plumb the depths of that creativity. He knew that to
fulfill our created purpose we would need to be innovative, developing new
tools and means of utilizing the resources and abilities that he had given to
us. In other words, obedience to God *requires* that we create technology.
This tells us that there is some inherent good in the technology we
create. Whenever we express our God-given creativity by coming up with
something that will help us be more fruitful, that will multiply and promote
human flourishing in a way that honors God, we act out of the *imago Dei*,
the "image of God" in which we were created. This is true whether or not
a person is a Christian or knowingly fulfilling God's design. God's common
grace, the grace that he extends to all people, whether they love and
obey him or despise and abhor him, empowers us to express our creative
impulses.

■ The Fall and the Curse

Yet the relationship between human beings and the technology they create
is not as simple as we would like to think. We know from the Bible that

soon after man was formed, he disobeyed God, altering the relationship between Creator and creation. Man was alienated from God, an enemy now, no longer a friend. Though man's relationship with God was disrupted by sin, and the world changed by God's curse, the mandate and the desire to create and multiply remained.

But it would no longer be easy.

The earth was no longer a friendly place for human beings. To the contrary, the natural world was now hostile and actively opposed to man. They would now have to fight for survival, utilizing every gift and ability that God had given them. In such a world — a world cursed by sin — technology becomes increasingly important, enabling human beings to regain some control over their lives and to fulfill their God-given dreams and desires. A sinless world had no need of medicine, but a fallen world required the development of medical and health *technologies* to enable human survival and flourishing. A sinless world had no need of weapons, but a fallen world required the development of weapons *technologies* for defense against animals and other human beings. A sinless world provided for their basic needs, enabling human beings to live in relative comfort and ease, but a fallen world required the development of *technologies* that would keep them warm and cool in hostile climates and herbicides that would prevent their crops from being choked by weeds. In a fallen world, technology enables human survival. It is all that stands between us and abject misery.

The Morality of Technology

So while it is true that we please and honor God when we create and develop new technologies, we must also understand that technology is like everything else in this sinful world: it is subject to the curse. The things we create can — and will — try to become idols in our hearts. Though they enable us to survive and thrive in a fallen world, the very aid they provide can deceive us with a false sense of comfort and security, hiding our need for God and his grace. Though the devices and tools we create are inherently amoral, at the same time we would be foolish to believe that they are morally neutral. The things we create to assist us in overcoming the consequences of the curse also seek to dominate us, drawing our hearts away from God rather than drawing us toward him in dependence and faith. That iPhone in your pocket is not an "evil" device. Yet it is prone to draw your heart away from God, to distract you and enable you to rely on your own abilities rather than trusting God.

It is difficult to try assigning any sort of inherent morality to individual technologies like the plow, the printing press, or the iPod. Even when we consider something like the technology behind nuclear fusion that created Tsar Bomba, we must recognize that the same technology that can level a city and kill hundreds of thousands can also provide power to that city—to its people, to its hospitals, enhancing the quality of life for its inhabitants. The same technology that allows doctors to operate on an unborn child, repairing its body within the womb, allows those doctors to also tear the baby from the womb. In other words, *it is not the technology itself that is good or evil; it is the human application of that technology.*

Thinking about technology in a distinctly Christian way means that we consider these three key ideas:

1. Technology is a good, God-given gift. Created in God's image, we have a mandate and a desire to create technology. Technology is the creative activity of using tools to shape God's creation for practical purposes.

2. Like everything else in creation, technology is subject to the curse. Though intended as a means of honoring God, our technologies often become idols and compound our sinful rebellion against our Creator.

3. It is the human application of technology that helps us determine if it is being used to honor God or further human sin. Discerning the intended use of a technology, examining our own use of it, and reflecting on these purposes in light of Scripture disciplines our technological discernment.

When we hold these together—when we understand our mandate, remember the consequences of the fall, and recognize the power of our own sinful desires in our use of technology—we are able to think about our technologies in a distinctly Christian way. We understand that Christians have the freedom and even the responsibility to engage in the development of technology and find creative applications for it in ways that further God's purposes. And yet we must still regard all technologies with a measure of suspicion, considering them with discernment, knowing that they easily prove to be a snare to our hearts. Christian philosopher Albert Borgmann strikes a helpful balance when he writes, "We should neither try to demolish technology nor run away from it. We can restrain it and must redeem it."[3] There is inherent good in creating technology. And yet there is inherent evil in abusing it or assigning it to a godlike prominence in our lives.

The Heart and Technology

We live with the harsh but undeniable reality that we are sinful people living in a world marked by God's curse. Technology presents us with a unique spiritual challenge. Because it is meant to serve us in fulfilling our created purpose, because it makes our lives easier, longer, and more comfortable, we are prone to assign to it something of a godlike status. We easily rely on technology to give our lives meaning, and we trust technology to provide an ultimate answer to the frustration of life in a fallen world. Because of this, technology is uniquely susceptible to becoming an idol, raising itself to the place of God in our lives.

Neil Postman, the late cultural critic and media theorist, pointed out that over time certain technologies come to be considered *mythic*, not in the sense of being fictional or legendary, but in the sense that they seem to have always existed in their current form. They have become part of the natural order of life. They become assumed, and we forget that they have not always been a part of our lives. Postman writes, "I have on occasion asked my students if they know when the alphabet was invented. The question astonishes them. It is as if I asked them when clouds and trees were invented. The alphabet, they believe, was not something that was invented. It just is."[4] We are all prone to the same error. We easily begin to think that the technologies that surround us—the devices, gadgets, and processes we take for granted—are a part of the natural world. "Cars, planes, TV, movies, newspapers—they have achieved mythic status because they are perceived as gifts of nature, not as artifacts produced in a specific political and historical context."[5]

As Postman points out, the alphabet has achieved mythic status in our culture, but what about the automobile and the telephone? Or the fact that television *always* has commercials and websites *always* have banner ads? Whenever we begin to assume "that's just the way things are and that's the way they've always been," we have stumbled on something of mythic power. For teenagers today, those who have been born and raised in a digital world, the television and the Internet are now mythic. A new generation is now unable to conceive of a reality in which instant worldwide communication does not exist. Yet just a few generations ago, having a real-time conversation with someone half a world away was only possible in the realm of science fiction.

When a technology has become mythic, we no longer view it as a strange outsider to our lives. We forget that it was invented by humans, that it was introduced into society by humans — humans who are just as limited, sinful, and shortsighted as we are. In fact, mythic technologies seem impossible to change. It seems easier to change ourselves and adapt to the new technology than to change it. Often, we assume that we *must* or *should* change to accommodate the new technology. We doubt that the technology could itself be the cause of a problem. We give technology the power to shape and change and fashion us, remaking ourselves in its image.

Consider the mobile phone. How easily we forgot that the cell phone and the pervasive communication it allows is a modern invention (or, as some would argue, a modern intruder into our lives). In the early 1990s, relatively few people owned a mobile phone, yet somehow those people survived! Today, the majority of us have a phone that we carry with us every waking hour, and we can barely imagine life without it. Already we are forgetting what life was like before the mobile phone, and we find ourselves thinking that it is a normal, natural thing to be able to contact one another at any time and in any place.

I was recently in the Dominican Republic, visiting some of the poorest homes in the poorest neighborhoods of Santo Domingo. And there, in a home without running water, a home that contained only the barest essentials, I saw two or three mobile phones. The mobile phone is a normal part of life as we know it today. And as a normal part of life it has begun to achieve mythic status in our culture. This means it falls outside of our normal social controls and our normal ways of thinking about technology. For instance, we may no longer consider it outrageous when a phone rings in the middle of a church service or when a person sends a text message from a funeral home. We are no longer outraged when someone interrupts a face-to-face conversation to accept a phone call or when a person spends an entire bus ride talking on his phone. Rather than changing the technology to fit our understanding of what is right and wrong, we change ourselves and our society's rules and mores, and we reshape ourselves in the image of the mobile phone.

What becomes mythic is only one step removed from becoming idolatrous.

▪ Idol Factories

I won't deny that I love gadgets. I've always had a soft spot for them in my heart, though by now I probably should have learned my lesson. At least half of the time when I buy a new gadget I quickly discover that I've wasted my money on something that serves no clear purpose in my life (the first laptop I owned, the first PDA, the first smartphone, the first …). I know that the Thursday newspaper brings with it the Best Buy catalog, and I always look forward to flipping through the ads to see what is new and what is on sale. As I look at that catalog, I find myself drawn to want gadgets and gizmos that just a few minutes ago I did not even know existed. I also find that many of the gadgets I purchase are adding noise and distraction to my life, and so I look for a new gadget or a new piece of software to solve the problems caused by my other devices.

This is something of a vicious circle. And I probably should have learned to resist the temptation by now. Yet when the latest and greatest device explodes into the national consciousness, when it is heralded as the wave of the future, the device to solve all of my problems, I still find my heart drawn to it. The allure of a new technology isn't simply the appeal of something shiny and bright, with buttons and lights. It's a desire that arises within my heart. And it can be incredibly powerful. It can be an idol.

Our idols like to hide from us, staying at a place in our hearts where we barely notice their existence. And yet, when we pause to consider their place in our lives, we simply cannot imagine life without them. Like the alcoholic who is surprised to find a bottle in his hand and yet who has no ability to throw that bottle away, we may find ourselves drawn and even addicted to technology, unable to imagine life without it. Not too long ago, in the dead of a frigid winter, I spoke at a youth retreat in northern Michigan. Before we left for the retreat, the pastor asked all the teens to leave behind their mobile phones, telling them that in order to properly "retreat" from the world for a time of spiritual reflection, they would need to forgo these devices. Very few of the students were able to give up their phones. Even as I spoke to them I could see several sitting in the audience with their heads down, quietly typing text messages to one another. It was clear that these students didn't really own their phones; they were "owned" by their devices, slaves to their desires and the satisfaction provided by this digital technology.

There is an unmistakable connection between technology and idolatry. John Calvin once remarked that the human heart is an idol factory. The heart is the seat of our emotions, our will, and our desire, and because of human sin and rebellion, it lies in direct opposition to God. The heart is eager to raise up new gods, putting other things and people in the place reserved for the one true God. Most of our idols are not simple objects of wood and stone, the kinds of images the ancient pagans used to bow before, believing these objects controlled weather patterns and enabled a good harvest. Instead, our modern idols reflect our inner desires for comfort, security, significance, and ultimately salvation. Tim Keller notes rightly that "anything can be an idol, and everything has been an idol."[6] Anything and everything, including that iPod in your pocket, your mobile phone, and your Wii.

So what exactly is an idol? Keller defines an idol as "anything more important to you than God, anything that absorbs your heart and imagination more than God, anything you seek to give you what only God can give." It is "anything so central and essential to your life that, should you lose it, your life would feel hardly worth living."[7] For some of us, power is an attractive idol. This was true for the first human beings, Adam and Eve, who chose to put themselves in the place of God, obeying their own impulses rather than the clear command of the Creator. And in that moment when they obeyed Satan rather than God, they made power into their personal deity. They elevated the power to know what God had wisely kept from them to a place of prominence in their hearts.

Our idols may be the craving of popularity or the lusting after illicit sex or the love of money or the power to control other people. We may even make an idol of technology in general, believing that innovation and human creativity hold the cure for humanity's ills. Or we may turn a specific type of technology into an idol in our lives—that mobile phone we simply cannot live without or a video game that consumes countless hours of our time.

When we give our lives over to idols, we hand them the keys to our heart. We become "possessed" by them, driven to use them, please them, and find our satisfaction in them. We become tools of our tools; rather than owning our gadgets we become owned by them. We begin to structure our lives around them, and our actions and choices are motivated by our need and desire for the blessings and benefits that idol provides for us.

Idols hide from us to avoid direct confrontation. And one of the ways they hide is by convincing us that they are actually good things in our lives. What makes this such an effective strategy is that many of the things that become idols in our hearts really are good gifts from God. But somehow they have become twisted and perverted into something evil. Money is a good gift from God that can be used to provide blessing and resources for those in need. Sexual intimacy is a gift from a loving Creator, given to draw a husband to his wife and a wife to her husband and increase their covenantal love for one another. Even power is a gift from God, given to maintain his moral rule through his servants. The trouble with each of these is not in the things themselves, but *in the position we give to them in our lives*. Each of these becomes an idol when we take something good and make it into something ultimate.

▪ Technology as an Idol

Because technology allows us to do what God created and called us to do, it can easily convince us that it is a good thing, something we should embrace and accept in our lives. And it certainly delivers on its promise, allowing us to live longer and cleaner and healthier and more comfortable lives. But because it is so effective in meeting our needs, it can easily begin to replace the one true God. We begin to think that it is the doctor or surgeon who heals us rather than the God who gives men wisdom to understand the inner workings of the human body. We begin to think that it is the mobile phone company that provides us with the blessing of communication rather than God's grace enabling families to stay in touch over long distances. We easily assume that technology has the power to grant us the benefits we desire, and we forget the Author of technology and the true purpose of our technologies—bringing glory to him.

Technology becomes an idol when we start to believe that humanity's hope, humanity's future, will be found in more and better technology. It becomes an idol when we place greater hope in technology than in God and when we measure human progress, not by the state of our hearts, but by new innovations in technology. Today we hear frequent claims about the amazing power of the Internet, that it will somehow bring all of humanity together in a global village where we will finally understand and love one another and stop fighting our petty wars. We often hear people promise that technology will solve all of humanity's ills, that somehow the latest innovation will right every wrong. In 2002, the National Science Foundation combined forces with the Department of Commerce to create a report that attempts to peer two decades into the future. They describe a wonderful world of technological utopia, free from the problems that plague our lives:

> Understanding the mind and brain will enable the creation of a new species of intelligent machine systems that can generate economic wealth on a scale hitherto unimaginable. Within a half-century, intelligent machines might create the wealth needed to provide food, clothing, shelter, education, medical care, a clean environment, and physical and financial security for the entire world population. Intelligent machines may eventually generate the production capacity to support

universal prosperity and financial security for all human beings. Thus, the engineering of mind is much more than the pursuit of scientific curiosity. It is more even than a monumental technological challenge. It is an opportunity to eradicate poverty and usher in a golden age for all humankind.[8]

How exciting to know that we are a mere two decades from accomplishing this grand vision: a human golden age that will be ushered in by the creation of amazing new machines! Here we have a heavenly vision of humanity—*but one devoid of God.* Technology has become our savior.

For technology to become a god in our lives, it does not require such a comprehensive commitment. We can make an idol of technology as we flip through the weekly advertisements, looking for something, anything, that will make our lives just a little bit better and fill the void in our hearts. The fact that technology is so effective is part of what makes it such an alluring idol. It delivers what it promises. For a while, at least.

▪ Technology as an Enabler of Idols

While technology can be an idol in and of itself, far more commonly it serves as an *enabler* of other idols. In this sense, technology has a secondary function, enhancing the power of an existing idol by strengthening its grip on our heart. Technology becomes a tool of our existing idols.

The man who makes sex into an idol, who is consumed by lust and who has no greater loyalty than following his sexual impulses, will use technology to enable and enhance his idolatry. His computer can certainly be used for many good and godly purposes, but instead it becomes a tool in the service of the idol that controls him, furthering his bondage, increasing the power of that idol through the viewing of pornography or the pursuit of illicit relationships. His cell phone, useful for communicating with loved ones, now becomes another conduit for a furtive glimpse at the pornography that fuels his lustful desire. His television, a possible means of education and relaxation, now becomes just another platform for perversion to enter his eyes and his soul. It is no coincidence that the explosive availability of pornography has happened alongside—and, more accurately, *through*— the digital explosion.

The woman who makes an idol of the love of money can now use her computer and her connection to the Internet to engage in online gambling, winning hundreds but losing thousands. She will use it to spend the money she makes and to fritter away the money she can't afford to be without.

A few years ago, I met a woman, a psychologist by training, who lived in a home that was stacked from floor to ceiling with boxes, bags, clothes, furniture, books and just about anything else you could imagine. A recluse who had given herself over to the idol of *stuff*, she spent her days using her computer to order more things over the Internet. She lived in squalor, her home crawling with rodents, narrow paths carved through her mountains of possessions. She spent her days and nights sitting and sleeping on a dirty old couch, surrounded by all of her stuff, miserable — a slave to her idol. Digital technology aided and abetted her idolatrous desire for possessions by giving her an easy, new way of buying things, objects that she hoped would give her the life she wanted.

This woman was a clear picture of the truth that our hearts are idol factories, constantly seeking new ways to usurp God's place in our lives. Yes, technology can be an idol in our hearts, one of the ways we replace God. But far more commonly, digital technology is a means to further the power of other idols. Technology, a good gift of God, is a gift that gets perverted and used to satisfy our selfish and evil desires.

If technology is so easily twisted and abused, our gut response may be to avoid it. We can try to carefully avoid using any form of digital technology, fleeing the temptation and the opportunities for evil they encourage. And yet for most of us, avoidance is not an option, nor is it necessarily the most biblical, God-honoring response, as we will see. Our task, then, is not to avoid technology but to carefully evaluate it, redeem it, and ensure that we are using it with the right motives and for the right goals. This is what we will seek to do in the second half of this book. We will look at a series of societal shifts that have come about through the digital explosion, uncovering the unique way in which these shifts feed the idol factory of the heart.

Before we get there, though, we need to take a small step — from the theological to the theoretical. We want to stop and reflect on what is always true about human beings and the technologies they create.

CHAPTER 2

UNDERSTANDING TECHNOLOGY

Most of us use many different kinds of digital technology every day, often unaware of their presence in our lives. Unless you are planning on running away to a deserted island to live as a hermit, you will likely spend a good portion of your life in the presence of digital devices. In fact, you may be using some kind of device at this very moment to help you read this book. Though these digital technologies often seem to seamlessly weave themselves into the fabric of our lives, we may have occasional moments when we have second thoughts. Have we perhaps grown a little too comfortable with digital technology, our fancy gadgets and beeping devices? Is there a hidden cost to using them, a price we must pay to enjoy their benefits? How exactly are these technologies changing us? And are these changes good?

People have long been wary of new technology—and often for good reason! In 1811, the owners of Nottinghamshire weaving mills began to receive angry and threatening letters from General Ned Ludd and his Army of Redressers. In truth, it's unlikely there ever was an actual Ned Ludd.

Historians now believe the name was fictitious, fabricated by workers in the textile industry. These workers, artisans who made their livelihood weaving fabric, were concerned about new technologies that were changing their industry. As England was becoming increasingly industrialized, machines had begun doing many of the jobs that had previously been done by men. The work of a skilled craftsman soon became the work of a machine operated by a mere apprentice or an unskilled woman. Wages plummeted—along with the quality of fabrics and even the very demand for quality. The craftsmen were quickly becoming obsolete and impoverished. While these new machines did inferior work, they were both fast and cheap—a trade-off most people were willing to make.*

Under the banner of Ned Ludd, the old artisans plotted to fight back against the factories that were bent on destroying their livelihood. They wrote threatening letters promising to destroy factories if they did not get rid of the machines. Not surprisingly, the factory owners refused to comply with their demands. And so the Luddites attacked. Within weeks, factory raids were a nightly occurrence and hundreds of knitting machines had been destroyed.

Luddism, as it became known, quickly spread from one county in England to the next. Soon the violence came to the larger cities of Yorkshire, Lancashire, and beyond. The government reacted by passing the Frame Breaking Act, a bill that made destroying machines a capital offense. The following year, seventeen men were sentenced to death for destroying textile machines. For several years, the violence continued, even leading to a pitched battle with government troops. But eventually, Luddism came to an end. It simply petered out. Faced with the overwhelming success of the new technology, the Luddites succumbed to the inevitable, unable to hold their ground against the forces of industrialization.

Today, *Luddite* is a disparaging term used to refer to a person who is opposed to or cautiously critical of technology. But it's important to remember that the original Luddites were not, in fact, opposed to technology per se. It was not the machines themselves that the Luddites feared and reacted against. Rather, they understood that technology is meant to serve humans, not the other way around. Luddites were not protesting the technology itself; they were objecting to the new economic realities brought about by the machines. In former times, craftsmen had

---

*This is still true today. It's why we buy our furniture from IKEA instead of from a local craftsman.

been able to work at their own pace and set their own prices for their goods. But with the dawn of industrialization and mass production, craftsmen fell on hard times and were increasingly forced to work for the hated factories. Suddenly they were answerable not to themselves but to a factory owner; they had to give up autonomy, or starve. They saw what the machines meant to their livelihood, to their lives, to their families, and to their communities. And they didn't like what they saw.

A Luddite in our world today is a person who fights against the use of technology. Luddites are cautious and wary about the supposed advantages of these digital devices. Deep inside, I think there is a little of the Luddite in all of us. Even those of us who live each day immersed in the digital sea have moments of awareness, times when we question what we are doing and what effect all of this is having on our lives. And our fears, if we are to name them, are not so much about the machines themselves. What we fear most are the *effects* of these devices on our lives and our families. Will these new technologies irrevocably change all that is dear to us, the things we value most?

With this in mind, let's look at five broad themes that help us understand the effects of any sweeping technological change—on human society and us as individuals.[1]

Technology Involves Both Risk and Opportunity

You may remember the anticipation and excitement surrounding the introduction of the Segway personal transporter vehicle. It was hailed as a device from the future, a vehicle that would change the world. Yet, though it offered a measure of innovation in the way it transported people, it really only provided an updated solution to an age-old question: How do I get from point A to point B? The device was evolutionary rather than revolutionary and, to this point in time, almost entirely inconsequential (unless you happen to be a mall cop).*

It is the rare technology that introduces something radically new and original to the human experience. Instead, most technologies simply promise improved ways of doing what we have always done. Whether a technology introduces something radical and revolutionary or simply

---

*And surely there is a parable in the fact that the owner of the Segway company was killed by one of his Segway vehicles when it drove him off a cliff.

provides a new solution to an old problem, one thing remains true: *every technology brings with it both risk and opportunity.* Every technology solves some problems while also introducing new ones; it opens up new opportunities even while imposing some new limitations.

Sometimes a technology can be used in two distinctly *different* ways, and in such cases the risk and opportunity are clear. For example, the forces of nuclear fission can power our homes through nuclear power plants; yet they threaten to destroy our homes through nuclear bombs. In other instances, the *same* use of a given technology carries with it both risk and opportunity. The television brought the world into our homes, allowing important news to spread faster than ever before and allowing families to share the experience of entertainment together. But even as it enabled these experiences, it advanced and fostered the understanding of news as entertainment and added a great deal of noise and distraction to our lives. Both the development of nuclear fission and the invention of the television had a benefit and a cost—a risk and an opportunity.

Coupled with this truth is a related one: We are prone to believe that new technologies offer us only good things. We find ourselves naturally drawn to the benefits and opportunities of new technologies but rarely pause to consider the risks. Advertisers lure us in with a long list of benefits and claims of better lives, but they only tell us half the story. We fall into this trap, time after time, for the simple reason that a technology tends to wear its benefits on its sleeve—while the drawbacks are buried deep within. The opportunities are obvious and apparent, while the risks are revealed only after close scrutiny and the slow march of time and experience.

Few would argue against the obvious benefits of the automobile. Cars have allowed our cities to grow, freed us to see more of the world, and given us opportunities to lead more mobile lives. And yet the automobile has also changed family structures; it has lead to hour-long commutes and cities choked with pollution. Along with the benefits have come costs, but it is always easier to focus on the benefits. The drawbacks have become evident only after decades of using this technology.

Sometimes the risks are known, but we choose to ignore them. Watch or read an advertisement for a new medication and you will likely hear a warning listing potential risks. You know the ads: after showing how a little pill will dramatically improve your life, you hear a fast-talking voice telling you how this same pill can have certain inconvenient and unexpected side effects—nausea, shortness of breath, dizziness, and death. Government regulations mandate that pharmaceutical companies inform consumers of both the benefits and risks of a product when they advertise. But our technologies offer no such warnings. The cell phone promised us instant connectivity, clear signals, and a measure of safety while traveling, but it gave us no warning label informing us that it would disrupt family life, ring at inopportune moments, or quickly grow out-of-date long before its contract was complete. Even worse, if the rumors are true, there is a possibility that our phones may end up increasing the incidence of brain tumors. In a similar way, the Internet promised families access to a world of knowledge and unparalleled communication opportunities, but this same technology has led to new forms of addiction, the exponential growth of available pornography, and a new form of violence known as cyberbullying. The risks were far more difficult to see.

So it is with every new technology. There are certainly benefits that we desire and would not want to live without. But such opportunities, clear to us from the beginning and often cleverly marketed to appeal to our desires, are always far easier to see than the inevitable costs. At the very least, this should teach us to cultivate a critical, cautious spirit whenever we learn of a new form of technology or are being sold the latest, greatest device to fix our problems.

The Medium Is the Message

The long history of human innovation proves that every technology has inevitable consequences. This is because every technology has embedded deep within it some kind of ideology. This is another way of saying that there are ideas that lie behind every technology that will make their way known over time. Neil Postman illustrates this with an example from Scripture:

> In Kings I [1 Kings 4:32] we are told [that Solomon] knew 3,000 proverbs. But in a culture with writing, such feats of memory are considered a waste of time, and proverbs are merely irrelevant fancies. The writing person favors logical organization and systematic analysis, not proverbs. The telegraphic person values speed, not introspection. The television person values immediacy, not history.[2]

Carried within the technology of writing and television are certain biases—fundamental ideas—that predispose us to see the world in one way and not another whenever we use these technologies. Such biases are, in some ways, the most important component of the technology because they will ultimately have the greatest impact on our lives. This is what Marshall McLuhan was alluding to with his now-famous aphorism "the medium is the message." McLuhan was encouraging us to look behind the technology and the capability of a given device to examine the ideas that underlie its use. He wanted us to know that both the person who invents a technology and the person who uses it are rarely able to see or identify the ideology behind it. Just as we tend to be initially blinded to the risk of a new technology, we find that we are similarly blinded when we try to discern the hidden message in our technology. Mark Federman, former chief strategist at the University of Toronto's McLuhan Program in Culture and Technology, warns, "We tend to focus on the obvious. In doing so, we largely miss the structural changes in our affairs that are introduced subtly, or over long periods of time."[3]

Like the risk inherent in a technology, the ideas that lie behind a given technology are often only apparent after time has passed and we have engaged in persistent and deliberate reflection. These ideas are often extremely influential, and they strike at the very heart of our human identity. We are inevitably shaped by the ideas our technologies carry within them.

But are we *merely* tools of our tools? Do our technologies ultimately determine who we are and what we will become? Philosophers have spilled much ink arguing about these subtle distinctions, about whether our technologies drive changes in humanity and human culture or technology remains an instrument in the control of human beings. As Christians, we have a third option, thankfully, and we can affirm that God is in control, firmly ordaining the course of human progress and societal transformation. Yet our confidence in God's purposes should not lead us to downplay or discount the fact that our technologies do, in fact, play a critical role in shaping our lives and our understanding of the world.

According to Mark Federman, the message of a new technology, the ideology carried within it, is "the change in inter-personal dynamics that the innovation brings with it."[4] So the "message" of a particular television show is not the show itself, with all its dramatic scenes and storytelling, but the change in attitude or the change in thinking that the audience experiences after watching it. The "message" of a show like *American Idol* may have been not the music but the nastiness of one of its judges—a nastiness that quickly shaped and defined society. The message within the medium of the Internet may not be the e-commerce sites and videos and blogs we use every day but the way humans are increasingly seeing themselves and their relationships with others in terms of *data* and *networks*. The true message of these digital technologies is buried deep inside them and will eventually be revealed in time. We will see their effect in the ways we think differently, act differently, and understand ourselves differently.

What we find, then, is that we only gain a measure of discernment about a medium after we've understood the message it carries with it—those usually unnoticed and nonobvious changes. We do not really understand *American Idol* until we understand how it has shaped us. We have not really understood a book until we've learned to recognize the ideologies buried deep within the words printed on paper and bound between two covers. The content of the book may be nearly inconsequential. The medium is the real message, the one that will change and affect our lives and our interactions with one another. We will not have understood the Internet until we've studied and understood the subtle messages it feeds our minds and our worldviews as we interact with it and use it day after day.

▪ Finding the Message

Obviously, this is not an easy task ahead of us. Some may wonder if it is even possible to discern the message hidden within a given technology. To live with virtue in this world, to use our technologies without being used by them, we must rededicate our efforts to look beyond what is most obvious. This will require a humble willingness to evaluate our own lives and compare the ways we are being shaped by a given technology with the life God envisions for us in the Scriptures.

Though McLuhan likely overstates his case (he was prone to more than a bit of hyperbole), we must still recognize that within every medium—every new technology—is a message that will inevitably work its way into our lives. McLuhan would likely warn us that reading the Bible on the screen of an electronic device is not the same as reading it on paper. He would tell us that singing hymns projected on a screen is not the same as singing hymns from a hymnbook. We tend to naively assume that a message stays the same, regardless of the medium we use to convey it, but McLuhan reminds us that the television screen, the page of a book, and the buzz of the headphone each has a unique message embedded within its use.

The challenge with a given form of technology is that we must seek to anticipate the changes that may result and respond to such changes with wisdom and discernment before they overtake us. McLuhan suggests,

"Control over change would seem to consist in moving not with it but ahead of it. Anticipation gives the power to deflect and control force."[5] The expert in martial arts is able to use the power of his opponent to deflect and control him, but only if he can anticipate what his opponent will do. In the same way, we can only react properly when we anticipate and have some measure of control over the technologies introduced into our lives.

Technology Is Ecological

When rabbits were imported to Australia in the middle of the nineteenth century, the result was more than a few cute little bunnies added to the continent—Australia + rabbits. Rather, the result was a whole new Australia, one in which entire species of plants were wiped out and in which erosion, caused by rabbits destroying vast areas of grassland, changed the very landscape. Just as adding a drop of poison to a glass of water changes the molecular structure of that entire glass, the addition of rabbits to the continent changed the entire ecology of the nation. Technological innovation is much the same. It is not additive but ecological. North America after the introduction of the telegraph was not simply the old North America plus the telegraph. Instead, it was a whole new continent. Today, we know that America plus the Internet is giving us a whole new nation, one that is radically different from the one before it.

The person who consumes technology is prone to believe that technology is a personal matter, that it can be added to our lives without any significant consequences. But here again, the insights of Neil Postman correct our thinking, pointing out that *technological change is not additive but ecological.*[6] In other words, it affects more than our lives as individuals. It introduces far more complex changes than anything we could have ever foreseen.

A technology changes the entire environment it operates in. It changes the way we perceive the world. It changes the way we understand ourselves. A person born into a print culture likely thought of himself as a book. Perhaps he would refer to himself as "an open book" when giving an interview. But a person born into an industrialized culture would likely think of himself as a machine, consuming food as fuel to keep the machine running. Such changes to our self-understanding are often impossible to undo. What's more, we are often oblivious to this kind of systemic change. The generation that spans these technological transformations may recognize that such changes are happening, but those who are born into them are blinded to them. A mother and father may anticipate some of the changes that will come to their family when they buy their first computer, but their children are born into a computer family. They never know life any other way.

Postman warns us that "the consequences of technological change are always vast, often unpredictable and largely irreversible."[7] That's a warning worth considering! If consequences are vast, unpredictable, and largely irreversible, we would do well to think very carefully before jumping in headfirst. And yet for some reason we are prone to be quite lazy in our thinking about technology. We regularly assume that the impact of a new technology is additive, that our lives will remain essentially unaffected by it. To counter this laziness in our thinking about technology, McLuhan proposes four questions that will help us identify the deep-rooted nature — and possible impact — of a new technology.[8]

1. What human trait, sense, or experience is *enhanced* by this new technology?

> This question encourages us to think about the ways in which a new technology will improve or enhance what already exists, to find the human function or sense that it magnifies or extends. We find that the mobile phone extends the human voice both individually and as a society, that the personal video gaming device extends the human hand and the imagination. We find that most of our digital technologies are created to enhance our ability to communicate.

2. What existing technology is made *obsolete* by this new one?

> Here we seek to find out what is likely to be replaced by a newer, improved technology. And we may also ask whether a given technology will disappear altogether or whether it will find a new niche, perhaps as art or artifact. The computer, for example, heralds the end of the television, rendering it increasingly obsolete, much as the automobile made the blacksmith unnecessary.

3. What old, abandoned technology does this technology *bring back to mind*?

> Here we ask whether there are old ways of doing things, old innovations that are called back into service by a newer technology. We may find that new ideas, new ideologies, call older ones back into relevance.

4. What unintended *opposite effects* might this technology have?

> Here we want to be able to see what consequences this technology may have that are directly opposite to its intended purpose. We look for contradictions, such as a device that promises greater levels

of communication while drawing us further away from face-to-face interactions with those closest to us (we don't know any devices that do this, do we? I'm looking at you, iPhone!). We may find that many of our digital technologies in claiming to enhance the human voice actually diminish it.

When we ask questions like these, we catch a glimpse of some of the ways in which a new technology affects us in an *ecological* sense, affecting us at a cultural and societal level. We see the human capabilities it enhances, the technologies it renders obsolete, the old paradigms it calls back to mind, and the way in which the actual consequences might contradict the intended use of the device. We think about how it might integrate itself into our lives. And we see how the ideologies present within the technology might shape us. Thinking through these questions equips us to think critically about technology so that we are prepared to respond to it.

Technology Shifts Power

I've often wondered if Johannes Gutenberg would ever have invented the printing press (or at the very least if he would have ever told anyone about it) had he known the effect it would have on the world and the consequences for his faith. Gutenberg, after all, was a faithful Roman Catholic, and historians believe that some of the first products he printed were actually indulgences — yes, those same indulgences that eventually sparked Martin Luther's criticism of the Roman Church and led to the Protestant Reformation. Though unintended, Gutenberg's invention forever changed the Catholic Church. The printing press was used by those pesky Protestant Reformers to print their seditious writings and their outrageous interpretations of the Bible. Martin Luther went so far as to call the press "God's highest act of grace." Even more important, the printing presses worked tirelessly printing copy after copy after copy of the Scriptures. For the first time in history, the words of God were available to everyone who wanted them. The cost of Bibles plummeted as their availability rose, and literacy soared. In just a few short years, the upstart Reformers had released Rome's stranglehold on Europe and, taking the people back to Scripture, pointed the way to a more faithful understanding of Christian doctrine. The world and the faith would never be the same. Had he been alive to see the result, I suspect Gutenberg would have been horrified.

Great shifts in power often follow hard on the heels of new technological innovations. At times this may be deliberate, as when a country introduces a powerful new weapon in order to intimidate its opponents. Indeed, this was the case with the U.S.S.R. and Tsar Bomba. They introduced this rather impractical weapon simply to flex their muscle. (How exactly did they intend to get that 52,000 pound, 50-megaton warhead over New York City anyway?) At other times, a shift in power may simply flow from the unpredictability of technology, as happened with the printing press. In either case, we see that the benefits of a technological change are not always evenly distributed across an entire society.[9] For example, think of the way that the printing press took power from the clergy and put it firmly in the hands of the laity. No longer would the clergy have a monopoly on reading, understanding, and explaining the words of God. Now every person could have his own copy of the Bible to read, to ponder, to digest, and to obey. The Roman Catholic Church would never recover the cultural dominance it had once enjoyed. Gutenberg, a faithful Catholic, never foresaw that his invention would cripple the church he loved.

So it is that the advantages and disadvantages of new technologies are not equally shared across society. There are always some who benefit—and some who lose. The blacksmith was rendered obsolete by the automobile, the telegrapher by the telephone operator. The words *computer* and *typewriter* once referred to specific people—an expert employee who performed a special task, not a machine. In each case, the machine defeated the man. Power shifted from the specialist to those who invented and embraced the new technologies.

We see similar shifts in power today. Those who were born before the dawn of the digital explosion often struggle to adapt to the new realities and are increasingly left behind. In the digital world, power has begun to shift from the old to the young. It is shifting from the expert to the amateur, from the printed word to the digital. Many of the old power structures are changing as an unintended consequence of digital technology. We saw a clear example of this in the 2008 United States presidential election when the Obama campaign harnessed the power of social media and new digital technologies, coasting to an easy victory. Because the McCain campaign did not understand the power of these new technologies, it failed to reach a critical segment of the population with its message. This segment, largely young and tech-savvy, gained power by becoming the swing vote in the election, pushing it firmly to a Democratic victory.

There is no surefire way of predicting the various ways in which a new technology will empower one segment of the population at the expense of another. At times the advantage goes to the early adopters, to those who grasp its significance and embrace it quickly, while at other times the advantage goes to those who resist the early allure and who, in doing so, save time and money that would otherwise have been wasted in pursuing a senseless innovation that was really nothing at all.

Though it is difficult to predict the winners and the losers and the ways in which power will shift, we are wise to remember that technology does bring shifts in power. We are wise to ask questions. We can ask whose interests are being promoted through a particular innovation. We can ask who will gain power through a given technology and who will lose power. As Christians, we are people who are subject to authority, and we must always take these changes in power and authority very seriously. We must seek to understand how digital technologies will reshape lines of authority both for our lives as individuals and for our life together as the church.

Technology Is Biological

We have seen that technology is ecological, that it does not just add itself to society but actually transforms an entire society. But scientists are only now beginning to understand a further truth: *technology is biological.* Our brains actually change in response to new technologies. The brain of a person raised in the age of print, a person who learned from books and who read books in time of leisure or study, has a brain that is markedly different from a person who has learned primarily from images or who has watched videos in times of leisure or study.

Scientists are discovering that the human brain, once thought to form in childhood and then remain largely unchangeable, is actually extremely malleable and sensitive to outside variables. Our brains are "plastic," able to bend and shape themselves. The brain of a person raised in a print culture is shaped by the dominant ideas inherent in print; the brain of a person raised in a digital culture is necessarily shaped by the dominant ideas inherent in the digital. This means that the brains of our children are not the brains of our fathers. Somewhere along the way, digital technologies, pervasive in the lives of our children, have shaped their brains in entirely new ways. And how could it be otherwise? By the time today's digital native reaches his twenties, he will have spent some 20,000 hours accessing the Internet and 10,000 hours playing video games. All of this digital immersion takes place during those formative years when the brain is developing, when it is very sensitive to any kind of outside influence.[10] His brain will be shaped by digital technologies, just as printed books shaped his father's brain.

Meanwhile, the digital explosion has even changed the way the adult brain functions. It has placed many of us into what has been described as a state of continuous partial attention, a state in which we devote partial attention to many tasks simultaneously, most of them having to do with communication. While we sit at our desks working on a report, we are also monitoring our mobile phones and our instant messaging accounts, giving partial attention to a host of different media. As we do so, we keep our brains in a constant state of heightened stress, damaging our ability to devote ourselves to extended periods of thoughtful reflection and contemplation.[11] After some time, our brains begin to crave this constant communication, finding peace in little else.

Pornography was once a secret vice but has now become a public passion and is nearly omnipresent on the Internet. Though once hidden, it is now a significant part of most teens' lives, carving new neural pathways, reshaping their very understanding of sex and intimacy. Ongoing exposure to pornography creates a "neurological superhighway" that traps men in a prison of their own lust. Escape from this trap is more than simply a matter of breaking an addiction; it involves rewiring the brain.[12]

As technology changes our biology, reshaping our brains, we become the product of our technologies in some deep and profound ways. A person who is raised on books becomes a person of the book, with a brain shaped by that medium. A person who is raised digitally becomes a digital person, with a brain shaped by the computer, the Internet, and the mobile phone.

Though this may sound alarming, it seems clear that this is consistent with the way God created us. We are molded and formed into the image of whatever shapes us. Here wisdom warns us that not all technologies are created equal in this regard. Each technology contains some kind of ideology, and the ideas in some technologies will be better than the ideas in others. This means that some brains will inevitably be "better" than others. The print brain may be superior to the digital brain in its ability to think and reason. But it may be that the digital brain is superior in other ways. What most concerns us is the fact that after five centuries, print is being supplanted by the digital. The print brain is being supplanted by the digital brain.

Technology is increasingly bumping up against the limitations of our brains and bodies, sometimes forcing rewiring or adaptation and sometimes causing overload and failure. Yet in the inevitable conflict between technology and biology, technology tends to find ways of winning simply because *we allow it to shape and re-create us at the deepest levels.* Though initially we have the upper hand and force our technologies to adapt to our desires, eventually we allow ourselves to be shaped by our use of them.

And so we have a basic structure for our technologies, a basic framework around which we can build a theoretical structure to understand this digital explosion. Our intellectual technologies always involve risk and opportunity, and typically we find it far easier to see the benefits than the potential drawbacks. We know that the medium is the message, that embedded deep within every technology are one or more ideas that will make their way out in time; that technology is not additive but ecological, changing the very structure of life and society; that technology shifts power; and that technologies cause biological change as the human body adapts to its most important influences.

With our theological and theoretical structures in place, let's look briefly at history to see how digital technologies came to be and how they came to play such a prominent part in our lives.

CHAPTER 3

A DIGITAL HISTORY

One of America's best-loved daughters, Laura Ingalls Wilder, was born in 1867 in the big woods of Wisconsin. Her Little House series of books stands as the consummate description of the life of a pioneer girl. These writings offer a fascinating glimpse into nineteenth-century life, life lived at the edge of the frontier. In several of her books, she describes what it was like to make long journeys, hundreds of miles in distance, across wild and unsettled lands. And in each of them, she describes what it was like to live in areas nearly untouched by civilization. The historical distance between Laura and us, between her pioneer life and our modern lives, is exactly what has made her writings so fascinating for generations of children.

Laura the pioneer girl died at the age of ninety in 1957, the same year that Russia launched a satellite (and a dog)* into space. She died only four years before humans orbited the moon and only twelve years before Neil

---

*The early history of space travel reads like a course in cosmic zoology. It's almost like the nations were competing to see who could send the largest and strangest menagerie into space.

Armstrong set foot on it. The year 1957 marked the dawn of the jet age, with the first flight of the Boeing 707, an aircraft that could make in just one hour the kind of journey that had taken her family months to complete. The world that Laura Ingalls Wilder was born into had ceased to exist long before she died. Her lifetime spanned the age of horse and carriage and the age of jet travel. She witnessed changes in every possible area of life. And as hard as it may be for us to believe, the pace of change has only quickened in recent years. The person born in 1957 who lives for ninety years will have witnessed change that is far greater, far more widespread, than that witnessed by Laura Ingalls Wilder.

Because we cannot understand who we are until we understand who we've been and where we've come from, we need to examine the history of the technologies that led us to our new digital world. We need to unpack the "story" of technology before the digital age, and we'll begin sixty-six years before Laura was born, at the dawn of the nineteenth century.

Digital Prehistory

In his account of the Lewis and Clark expedition, historian Stephen Ambrose notes, "A critical fact in the world of 1801 was that nothing moved faster than the speed of a horse. No human being, no manufactured item, no bushel of wheat ... no letter, no information, no idea, order, or instruction of any kind moved faster. Nothing ever had moved any faster." For all the benefits and advances America enjoyed it was "a society whose technology was barely advanced over that of the Greeks. The Americans of 1801 had more gadgets, better weapons, a superior knowledge of geography, and other advantages over the ancients, but they could not move goods or themselves or information by land or sea any faster than had the Greeks or Romans."[1] Though they lived eighteen hundred years after Jesus, they could make their way across America no faster than Jesus had made his way across ancient Palestine.

Pause for a moment to consider such a world. These were the days when the journey from Boston to New York took three days; when it took Thomas Jefferson ten days to go from his home in Monticello, Virginia, to Philadelphia, Pennsylvania, a distance that today we can drive in a morning; when crossing from the Old World to the New took several long and dangerous weeks. The adventuresome ones who later in the century chose to follow the Oregon Trail from Missouri to the West Coast would consider themselves blessed if they could make the journey in less than six months' time.

Information moved just as slowly and with no guarantee that a message sent had actually been received. In January 1815, during the last battle of the War of 1812, hundreds of men were killed and over two thousand wounded or taken prisoner, even though the war had officially ended almost two weeks prior. It would take until February for news to reach the troops that a treaty had been signed on December 24. All those lives had been lost in vain, fighting a war that had ceased. Even by 1861, in the days of the Pony Express, the fastest riders on the swiftest horses would still require ten days to carry a message from St. Joseph, Missouri, to Sacramento, California, some 1,900 miles distant. It would be ten days more, at least, before the person sending the message could expect a reply. And this was the *express* (and prohibitively expensive) route.

A radical transformation was afoot.

The Information Age

Beginning in the middle years of the nineteenth century, the steam engine forever transformed travel. For the first time in human history, people could move faster than the horse. The "iron horse," as the locomotive was known, began to tirelessly take people across the nation far faster than any horse could run. Even the first rudimentary locomotives were capable of traveling at 20 or 25 miles per hour. While the United States boasted only 40 miles of rails in 1830, just ten years later it had increased to almost 3,000 miles, and ten years after that, it was narrowing in on 10,000. By the end of the century, America had well over 160,000 miles of rails, and this in a nation that is 3,000 miles across. Goods, people, and information could now move at unprecedented speeds. Information was about to catapult ahead.

In 1844, Samuel Morse, using a telegraph, famously tapped the words of Numbers 23:23, "What hath God wrought!"* through 37 miles of cable stretching from the Old Supreme Court Chamber in the U.S. Capitol in Washington, D.C. to Mount Clare Station in Baltimore. As he did so, he inadvertently kicked off the Information Age. Morse's great advance was not in the telegraph itself, since as a technology it had already been proven. Rather, his contributions were in creating a standardized system

---

*Many people add a question mark at the end of this phrase as if Morse meant to ask "What hath God wrought?" But Numbers 23:23 uses these words as an exclamation, "What hath God wrought!" This is an exclamation about the power of God. These words had been chosen by Annie Ellsworth, the young daughter of one of Morse's friends.

of communication using his alphabet of dots and dashes and in creating a receiver that would emboss those dots and dashes into a ribbon of paper, thus creating a permanent record of the transmission.

The telegraph offered people a way to communicate quickly over long distances, and it caught on fast. Within two decades, almost all of America was wired, and cables even stretched across the Atlantic Ocean, linking whole continents in what one historian has termed "the Victorian Internet."[2] India was connected by 1870, and Australia by 1872. Families, friends, nations, and continents were bound together in a completely new way. It changed virtually everything.

Business and crime, social interaction and romance, war and diplomacy — the breadth of the impact was remarkable. Barely any area of life or society remained untouched by this amazing new technology.

After thousands of years of near stasis, the world had suddenly become radically smaller. Military commanders who had always sent orders by horse, often waiting weeks or even months for a reply, could now communicate instantly with troops a continent away. Small-town newspapers that had once written of little more than local events, with occasional bits of stale national news mixed in, were now able to report on international events almost as they were happening. It is no coincidence that the Associated Press news agency was founded just four years after Morse sent his first telegram.

At the dawn of the information age, many criminals, both petty crooks and organized rings, operated within train stations. They knew they could rob and steal and then immediately hop aboard a departing train. Since nothing moved faster than a train, they were assured of a clean getaway. After the telegraph appeared on the scene, a criminal would often find the police waiting for him as the train pulled into the station down the line. Foreshadowing our own Internet romances centuries later, there are even stories of "online" romances, where a man and woman would meet and court and sometimes marry — all through the telegraph! Localized dialects developed in which telegraphers created short forms of common words and phrases in order to save time and ease communication.

With the newfound ability to send information so quickly and so inexpensively, the new problem of information overload suddenly appeared. Where local news was once the mainstay of the newspaper, suddenly every paper across the country was expanding to carry pages and pages of national and international news. No longer was it necessary for every story to be local for it to be relevant to the reader. Businessmen would find themselves being interrupted in their homes—long after office hours—with rush telegrams arriving at their front door (a precursor to the way we now experience the constant ringing of our mobile phones). For decades, the world sought to understand how to best deal with this revolution in information. It took many years to adjust and develop social customs, etiquette, and ways of dealing with the new realities brought about by the new technology. In fact, it took just long enough for the telegraph to fade into history, only to be replaced by its successor, Alexander Graham Bell's telephone (a device whose growth outpaced even that of the telegraph). And so the adjustment process began once again.

The telegraph had changed not just the medium of communication but the message itself, our very conception of *information*. Until the telegraph, information was valued for its ability to assist in understanding and solving particular problems. It was relevant for its ability to be a means toward a greater end.[3] Information tended to be of local interest. What was useful information in one town would garner virtually no interest in the next. But in the age of telegraphy, information became an end in itself and was increasingly disengaged from context or locale. Suddenly, distance was no longer a constraint or a consideration; information could move across the continent with all the ease it took to spread across town. The telegraph had begun to tie the world together into a cohesive whole, where town was bound to town by common information. That cable tied them together, both literally and figuratively. As it bound towns together, it changed the unique identity of individual communities, making one town remarkably like another as each fed on the same diet of information and shared events. Even as the telegraph made people feel less isolated and developed communal identity around common experiences and shared knowledge, it also began to eliminate those features that had made each community different.

Information also became a commodity. No longer was it simply useful as a resource to solve a problem; information became a good in itself. Its value was not in its usefulness or applicability but in the speed with which it could be communicated and the level of human interest it contained. The telegraph's value was not that it could analyze information or separate out the relevant from the irrelevant. It simply moved information quickly and in large quantities.

Gone was the idea of news as "functional information."[4] Very quickly arose the notion of news as entertainment. Instead of newspapers filled with in-depth analyses of local affairs, consumers demanded papers filled with interesting but irrelevant snippets of information, often from faraway places. "News from nowhere, addressed to no one in particular"[5] gave people much to talk about but little to act on. It entertained and outraged, but demanded no response, no action. Neil Postman writes about the great loop of impotence this created: "The news elicits from you a variety of opinions about which you can do nothing except to offer them as more news, about which you can do nothing."[6] People knew lots of facts, but had intimate knowledge of very little. Their knowledge *about* the world far surpassed their knowledge *of* the world.

The speed of this transformation, this information revolution, was breathtaking. In the span of a century the horse, which for thousands of years had been the mainstay of both transportation and information, was forgotten, reduced to a quaint form of entertainment. As the Pony Express rider galloped past the telegraph poles being laid from the East Coast to the West, he galloped into his own demise. The world would never be the same again.

There was no turning back.

But this was only the first chapter — possibly the preface — to what would later become "the next story," the story of our digital world. If the telegraph had made the world radically smaller and changed our very conception of information, the television would take us from a culture dominated by words to a culture dominated by images. It would introduce us to a new medium that would soon be found everywhere — the screen.

The Rise of the Image

There was a time, not so very long ago, when we did not have screens in our homes. Those who wanted to watch a movie reel of the latest news would have to go to a cinema, and there they would see the shaky black-and-white images and hear the dramatic voiceovers. "December 7, 1941. A day of infamy. Even as Japanese diplomats were conferring with Secretary of State Hull on peace measures, Nipponese planes were swooping down on Pearl Harbor." Five years later, in 1946, only 1/2 of 1 percent of American households had even a single screen in their home.

But by 1999, a mere fifty-three years later, a prominent researcher was able to declare that "watching TV is the dominant leisure activity of Americans, consuming 40 percent of the person's free time as a primary activity."[7] And that percentage increased to north of 50 percent when it included the time spent watching television as a secondary activity—while eating or talking or doing something else. By the late 1990s, the average American home had a television on for more than seven hours per day, and individuals averaged between three and four hours a day staring at that screen.

Just ten years after that, an average adult was found to be spending nearly nine hours per day in front of some type of screen (or, more accurately, a near-endless succession of screens). About a quarter of his time was spent in the presence of at least two screens, and sometimes three or more.[8] After all, why waste time watching television when you can waste time watching television, surfing the web, *and* sending text messages—all at once! Television consumption had climbed slightly, but added to it was the time spent in front of a computer, at work and at home, time spent on a mobile phone, and time playing some type of video game.

It does not take a lot of imagination to realize that such profound shifts are bound to impact our lives, both as individuals and as a society. As we have learned, like every media, television carries with it certain embedded ideas. The media itself says something more important than the message it happens to convey at any given moment. There are deep and profound ways in which we are being shaped by the television and the computer screens, and these are made even more significant by our dedication and near-total devotion to the visual medium.

After the invention of the television, the world quickly transitioned from a print-based culture to an image-based culture. The image was soon favored over the power of the printed word. Where people had once believed what they *read*, they would now only believe what they *saw*. Where once words had conveyed truth, that truth was now being shared through pictures and video. Today we take it for granted that a picture is worth a thousand words, if not more. But it was not always this way.

Images communicate in a way that is very different than words. The initial impact of an image is not so much a *thought* as it is a *feeling*. Look at a newspaper from the nineteenth century, and you'll find advertising that describes a product using words. Today you're likely to find images that create a feeling and elicit an emotional response. The human brain processes images and words in completely different ways. The word is processed by the brain's left hemisphere, the area that deals with logic, sequences, and categories. The image is processed in the right hemisphere, the realm of intuition and holistic perception, not linear analysis. An image is processed in an instant, while words take time and sequence.[9]

As we consider this transition from the word to the image, we must look beyond the pictures themselves. Whether I learn about "lions" through images or words, it is true that I am still learning content. But I am prone to miss that the medium itself is subtly changing the way that I think. The change from word to image is reprogramming my brain. "The television image is extraordinarily stimulating to the brain, and not in a healthy, 'this discussion about politics is so *stimulating*' way—more like the sugar-is-stimulating-to-the-body way. The televised brain candy we consume doesn't develop—or even require—any mental capacity."[10] Learning through images and visual media is directly opposed to learning by reading, which requires a more sustained focus and actually generates new skills and capacities in the brain.

This makes television an ideal medium for amusement. While the message of a particular program can be deadly serious, the medium itself is all about entertainment. After a time, even serious content will come packaged as a form of entertainment, a fact we regularly encounter in news broadcasts. The very worst news is only a brief segue from something fantastically light and amusing.

This is also clearly seen in the way politics has changed over the years. Political discourse, once shaped by speeches and debates, is now driven by sound bites and images. It is almost impossible to conceive of a truly ugly person rising to the office of president of a nation today. Though he may be brilliant and can say all the right things, he will not pass the image test. His picture speaks a thousand words, more powerfully than anything he can say or write.

Television brought the screen into our homes. What was once novel and interesting in the cinema took its place in our living room, in the center of the house, replacing the fireplace. The family now gathered around the television to share common experiences: the World Series, the moon landing, a presidential assassination. The television became the medium of the common culture, a medium that bound us together.

Television has taken us from a culture that learned from print, was entertained by print, was persuaded by print, and trusted print to a culture that now relies on the image. *It has changed our perception of ourselves and our understanding of the world around us.* Television represents more than flickering images on a screen. It gives us a new identity. A new ideology. A new idolatry.

The second chapter of the "next story" was being written as the components for a truly digital world began to fall into place. The television continued what the telegraph had begun, shrinking the world and adding to our lives a new medium: the screen. We were growing dependent on images.

Just a few more chapters remained to be written.

The Dawn of the Digital

Television reigned from the 1950s until the dawn of the twenty-first century. But in the early 1970s, the eventual rival to the television began its ascendancy: the personal computer. The introduction of the personal computer marked the start of a radical divide within our society, one that would divide young from old and one that will persist for several decades. There are many who still remember the world before the dominance of digital technology. And yet there are many others, of younger generations, who have never known anything *but* a world dominated by digital technology. Their world has been (and always will be) digital. Older generations are now digital *immigrants*, having been forced to transition from the old world into the new. Younger generations are digital *natives*, for whom digital technologies are like the air they breathe—a simple and unremarkable feature of the world they live in.[11]

▪ Digital Immigrants

Though bulky, archaic computers had existed for decades, it was only in the latter years of the 1970s that they became both small and affordable. The Apple, the Commodore, and the PC all made their debut sometime between 1976 and 1981. Slow, clunky, expensive, and laughably underpowered from our twenty-first century perspective, these computers were revolutionary for their time. They achieved what many had thought impossible—they brought the power of the computer to the masses, into the home.

If you were born prior to 1980, as I was, you were a witness, though perhaps an unwitting one, to all of these changes. Like me, you are a digital immigrant. You were born and spent some of your life in a pre-Internet, pre-digital world and have had to immigrate into this new reality. You remember what life "used to be like" and how things were different. You remember mailing letters to pen pals instead of e-mailing them; you remember being "out of touch" with someone because your phone was physically connected to the wall and couldn't follow you into the car; you remember using an encyclopedia that took up an entire shelf in the local library; you remember card catalogs and cassette tapes and "laptop" computers that were far larger and heavier than any lap could ever hold. Perhaps you even learned to type the way I did—on a manual typewriter that needed no electricity to function and had no backspace key.

For you there is likely a sharp contrast between life *before* and *after* the digital explosion, and there remains a sharp contrast between life *online* and life *offline*. These two experiences are very different and distinct in your mind. The offline world is where you live day-to-day, while the online world is a destination where you go to e-mail or shop or get the news.

▪ Digital Natives

If you were born after 1980, you are a digital native. The world as it exists today is the only world you've ever known. You may remember a time when mobile phones were rare, the exception more than the rule, but then again, maybe your memory goes no further than the old flip phones that were all the rage once upon a time.

For you, there may be no great or important distinction between life *online* and *offline*. Your identity in the digital realm and your identity in the world of flesh and blood are one and the same. You may have different representations of that identity, but you make little distinction between them. You move seamlessly between face-to-face interaction and digital interaction through messaging or e-mail. In fact, you may prefer digital interaction, finding the face-to-face somehow unnatural or intimidating. Your mobile phone is a part of who you are, and without it you feel like the world is moving on without you. You enjoy television and surfing the web, and especially enjoy doing two or three of these things simultaneously. You can switch back and forth between them as easily as you can change your socks.

You don't know what a card catalog is and may never have heard of *Encyclopedia Britannica*. Wikipedia is your first stop when doing research, though you've often been warned by people older than you that it's not trustworthy. You barely remember compact discs, not to mention cassette tapes. This is your world, and you are comfortable in it.

▪ The Growth of the Computers

Though initially hailed as a technology for the workplace, it did not take long for developers to harness the power of the computer for entertainment and communication. Games, first text-based but soon utilizing images, grew up as a powerful new industry, initially using specialized console hardware, then expanding to generic computers as well. No sooner had the computer appeared in the home of hungry consumers than they wanted to link their computers to interact with one another. Rudimentary bulletin board systems were the early answer, then Usenet, and eventually the World Wide Web.

By the year 2000, more than 50 percent of households had at least one computer, and 42 percent of them were connected to the Internet.[12] No longer was the computer a device used primarily for business; it was a device used for both business and pleasure, wrestling with spreadsheets and storing the family photos, typing business e-mails and chatting with friends through instant messengers. It had become an indispensable device in all areas of life—business, education, and pleasure.

As the old century faded into the new, social media software began to appear—blogs, Facebook, MySpace—and it, too, soon came of age, giving hundreds of millions of users a new way to connect, share, interact, and gossip.

All the while, computers became much smaller and exponentially more powerful. What was once the size of a room could now easily fit inside your pocket. Portability became the order of the day, with laptops, then netbooks and tablets, dominating the marketplace. The laws of capitalism dictated that prices would fall, and indeed, they did, so that what once cost tens of thousands of dollars could eventually be manufactured for next to nothing.

Here at the dawn of the second decade of the twenty-first century, the lines between the television and the computer are growing increasingly blurry. Televisions serve as computer screens; computers now serve as televisions. Television is now broadcast over the Internet, and computer games are played on TV screens. Though television continues to be the most popular form of entertainment, it is increasingly being absorbed into the overall computer experience.

As computers matured and began to dominate our culture, they were accompanied by a near-endless number of related devices. This was brought about by a series of technological developments. Storage became radically less expensive to the point that it became more costly to erase information than to simply keep it and buy more storage. Computers increased in power as manufacturers found ways to increase processing speed. Computers grew smaller as their components were miniaturized, and new communication media arose—cellular networks, global positioning satellites, and, most important of all, the Internet.

As the first computers found their way into the eager hands of consumers, so also did mobile phones. And as the computer developed steadily, becoming all the more powerful, cost-effective, and mobile, so too did the phone. Once a device reserved only for businessmen who needed to be connected during their commute, it soon found its way into the hands of every teenager, becoming something of a rite-of-passage, coming-of-age device. More than a simple "telephone," it quickly established itself as a part of a person's very identity.

Gaming consoles also grew in power and reach, with different devices establishing niches among the very young all the way to the very old. The age of computer gamers rose steadily so that by 2009 the average age was thirty-four.[13] Digital cameras became less expensive and more powerful and were soon integrated into cell phones. e-Readers finally began to live up to their promise, with new e-ink technology that adequately mimicked the age-old experience of reading on the printed paper. iPods and MP3 players sold in the hundreds of millions, adding sound tracks to our lives. Soon all of these functions were being combined into powerful multifunction devices that, twenty years ago, were only found in the realm of science fiction. Just four decades after their introduction, computers had become dominant within the home. Their impact on business and education, and almost every other area of life, was equally as powerful.

Along the way, though, a subtle transformation also occurred within us. We began to think of ourselves in computer terms. We spoke of *information* as if life and the universe itself, at heart, is a collection of data. We began to think of our brains as central processing units (CPUs), increasingly using the terms we had learned from the computing world to discuss biological functions. We exported our memories to hard drives, eventually trusting the data on the disk more than we trusted our own minds.

As we began to give our thoughts and our memories—our very identities in many cases—over to computers, we allowed them to do more and more things that could have been done in other ways. We found that if we could have it done by computer, we *wanted* it done that way. And eventually we began to forget how to do certain things without a computer. We made computers our slaves but found that in our reliance on computers we had also become slaves. For all that they did for us, we found ourselves growing increasingly dependent on them. We began to wonder: Who is really in control? Who owns whom?

One final chapter remained in our story. We had the technology and our growing reliance on computers. What was missing was a network that would tie it all together.

The Conquest of the Digital

Though advances in technology had greatly changed our lives, the *conquest* of the digital was made possible by the development of the Internet. Here at last we had found a means of binding together all of our devices. Here we had discovered a way of extending a persona across our gaming, social, working, and even worshiping communities. The Internet unifies the identity of a person across time and space, but it also binds device to device and person to device.

One obvious but profound change that came with the development of the Internet was its ability to make communication a two-way affair. A book is a one-directional medium. An author writes a book; a publisher prints it to paper; and the reader is able to read it (as you are doing right now). What the author *cannot* do is reply within that medium or interact with you or with other readers. Television is much the same. It is broadcast over the air and received by the viewer. That viewer, though, does not interact with the show. Rather, he experiences it and moves on to the next thing. The Internet, though, introduced the ability to interact in a more complete way. We can both download *and* upload; we can read *and* write; we can consume *and* create. The medium of the Internet has democratized information, making it accessible in a completely new way.

In its infancy, the Internet was hailed as a word-based medium, a literary medium that would restore the dominance of the word. Hopeful philosophers saw in it the promise of undoing the damage of television and its never-ending parade of images. Such hope sounds quaint and naive today. In the early days of the web, it was slow, difficult to navigate, and mostly devoid of images. Early on, it did indeed hold some promise for those who were mourning the downfall of the word. But times quickly changed, and philosophers' hopes have waned. Vastly improved speed and greatly increased bandwidth have made images, sounds, and video the dominant media on the web. Meanwhile, the text has continued to suffer, with studies showing that, at best, Internet users skim text rather than read it. In fact, "skimming" is now the dominant metaphor for reading. Though words are a crucial part of the online experience, they bow before the gods of visual and audio media.

Certainly, words have not been entirely removed from the digital realm. We are now on the cusp of a great transformation in reading. For centuries, people have prophesied about the end of the book—but time after time they have been mistaken. They have seen the arrival of media that would *displace* the book and have assumed that these new media forms would *replace* the book. We have seen that while television drew society away from the book, it could never carry content in the same way as a book could. Thus it never stood a fair chance of actually replacing the book. But today we have digital devices that can carry text in a digital format and do so with some degree of excellence. Amazon's Kindle, first released in 2007, very quickly rose to prominence and has been followed by a host of similar devices, already selling in the millions. Though the printed book will likely remain with us for some time, it seems likely that its days are now, finally, numbered.*

The Internet dwarfs even the printing press in its impact on human culture, in its rate of adoption, in its immediate impact. Though from our narrow and shortsighted perspective we are now beginning to see this, we know that only as time passes will we fully understand how it has shaped and transformed our lives.

So here we sit today, surveying the landscape after the digital explosion. We live in the glare of screens; we outsource our memories to bits and bytes; we experience some of our deepest and most important relationships through ethereal networks powered by electricity and computer hardware. We are a digital people—a digital generation, dependent on our devices.

And the era of digital dominance has only just begun.

We are left wondering what changes remain, what will come next. We are just beginning to wonder how the digital devices in our lives are beginning to change us. We are starting to see that though we made these technologies in our image, they are eager to return the favor. And so, as we turn to the second part of this book we will unpack six ways in which our lives, our churches, and our society have been changed because of the digital explosion. And we'll begin to think more clearly about what it means to live with virtue, faith, and discernment in this digital age.

---

*The printed book won't ever disappear altogether, but it is already declining. Some day in the near future, the printed book will have less market share than the digital book. In the more distant future, it may be only special editions of books that actually go to print.

Talk to Your Tech

We have now looked at technology through three different lenses—the theological, the theoretical, and the experiential. Before we move to Part 2, let's see how we can try to live within that sweet spot between the three circles. Perhaps you are finding that you are fed up with the constant distraction of your cell phone, or perhaps you find yourself checking e-mail compulsively in the office, at home, in the car, at the dinner table. Perhaps you are about to head to the mall to buy that new gizmo, that new gadget you have heard so much about.

We know that technology is a good gift of God and one we are free to use if we can use it for his glory. But we know as well that technologies bring both risk and opportunity, that we tend to focus on the benefits while ignoring the risk, that we tend to think technology is additive rather than ecological, that we tend to see only its most immediate impact in our lives and in society. And in this light our task becomes clear: We need to seek to understand how a technology will change and shape us *before* we introduce it to our lives. We cannot afford to be so shallow as to think that we can enthusiastically embrace a new technology without eventually suffering from at least some of its drawbacks. We can almost always see the immediate benefits but we are wise to dig deeper, looking for the inevitable consequences.

What we need to be willing to do is to ask questions of our devices. We need to talk to our technology, to ask questions of it and not rest until we understand the answers. These are questions to ask when society transitions to a new technology; they are questions to review with our children when they suggest they are ready for their first computer or mobile phone; they are questions to ask ourselves when we find our hearts and minds drawn to the latest and greatest device.

▪ *Why Were You Created?*

A technology will eventually and inevitably do what it was created to do. Yet we, the consumers, rarely know exactly what the technology was created to do. If we can find the original purpose for a technology, we will not be surprised when we learn how it will soon begin to change and shape us. If a technology was created for military applications, we will not be surprised that it treats us like soldiers. If it was created for use in a hospital, we will not be surprised to find that it treats us like doctors. When we understand that cellular phones were introduced to keep businessmen in touch with the office while they were away from it, at home or on the road, we will not marvel that our mobile phones tend to do just that—to keep us in touch when we would rather escape. The phone is simply doing what it was created to do.

The pessimist might say that every new technology is heralded as a means of addressing some great problem but in the end is quickly taken over by the entertainment industry. That person might not be far from the truth. Television was not originally heralded for its value as entertainment, and yet today this is almost all it is, whether we are watching sitcoms or reality television or whether we are watching the news (which is largely a form of entertainment—it is news *as* entertainment). This may not be always true, but it does point us to an important reality: there are unintended consequences to our technologies. When we create a new technology or add one to our lives, we may have a sense of how it will play out its hand, but rarely do things go exactly as we had planned. More often than not, the consequences are quite different from what we had expected.

This owes, at least in part, to the reality that the invention of a technology almost always precedes its function. Technology is generally created independently from the way it will eventually be used. It is usually only after a new technology is invented that we use our creativity and ingenuity to find ways of integrating it into our lives. This exacerbates its unintended consequences. If a technology was created specifically for business application and we adapt it to a worship service, we will see that there are some businesslike ideologies wrapped up in that technology (such as when we take PowerPoint from the boardroom to the sanctuary).

The wise consumer of technology will realize that the technology he uses today, the technology he has come to love and depend on, will have unintended consequences in his life and in the world around him. He will look not just to the technology itself but to the function for which it was created, the problem it was originally supposed to address.

- **What Is the Problem to Which You Are the Solution, and Whose Problem Is It?**

Neil Postman proposes that we ask of any new technology, "What is the problem to which this technology is a solution?" Assuming that we add new technologies to our lives to help us solve life's problems, whether those are problems of comfort or dominion, Postman suggests we think carefully about what we hope to accomplish with or through any technology. It is a good and fair question, an obvious one even, yet we too often choose to ignore it.

When we ask what problem a technology is seeking to address, we begin to understand how it will play out its hand in our lives. We may even find that a great new technology is a solution to something that no normal person would even consider a problem. We may find that what the manufacturer of a device considers a problem, or wants *us* to consider a problem, is utterly meaningless. It may be that the problem has been manufactured simply to convince us of our need for a certain product (which reminds me of the Snuggie, the blanket with sleeves. Is there anyone in the world who actually *needs* a Snuggie? It is a classic example of a solution to what was not really a problem—something that is true, I think, of the majority of "As Seen on TV" products.).

Once we have identified the problem we should also ask: Whose problem is it? In almost every case, a new technology will solve some kind of a problem, but it may not be *our* problem. It may be that a great new device does not solve any problem in my life, but my purchase does solve the manufacturer's falling annual profit. It may be that someone else will see all the benefit brought about by this new innovation while I assume all the cost, whether that cost be in finances, time, or distraction.

- **What New Problems Will You Bring?**

By asking the first two questions, we have learned why a technology was created, and we have understood what problem it seeks to solve and whose problem it really is. Now we want to ask a natural follow-up: If we decisively solve this problem, what new problems may we have created and who may we have harmed? Here we must stop and pause to consider what new problems will arise as a result of our adoption of this technology. And we want to see who will be most affected by these new problems.

We may well find that in adopting a new all-in-one mobile phone—one that allows us to leave the office a little bit earlier while staying in greater touch with our clients—we have created the new problem of overload through distraction. We find that we can now never escape from the torrent of communication and information flowing out of it. Or perhaps we find that we are spending more time with phone than with family, harming our most important relationships. We've created problems related to information overload and distraction, and while we are harmed by it, it is our families that are most affected. While the new technology solved some problems, it could not do so without creating others.

▪ What Are You Doing to My Heart?

This final question is one that all Christians will want to ask when evaluating a new technology, and especially a new digital device. Here we turn back to the issue of idolatry and ask whether this device is itself a kind of idol. Am I running out to buy a device so I can be the first one in my office, school, or church to own the device? What is it that draws me to the device, and when I look beneath the surface, why do I *really* want it?

And even if this device is not an idol in and of itself, I ought to ask whether it is going to increase the power or control of another idol. Perhaps I am controlled by my desire to remain in constant touch with e-mail, and this device will allow me to check my e-mail more often and in more places. Or maybe I am controlled by a desire to find bargains, and this device will allow me to monitor more deals, more auctions, more sales. In both cases, this device will serve to feed my idols, to care for them, to enhance their power in my life. Again, I need to ask why I *really* want this device. There may be a host of reasons, both good and bad.

PART 2

CHAPTER 4

SPEAKING, TRUTHING, LOVING, LIVING
(Communication)

It was the old British war hero Admiral Lord Nelson who declared that every man became a bachelor once he was beyond Gibraltar. Gibraltar—that giant chunk of rock that juts into the mouth of the Mediterranean Sea, guarding against anyone who would want to sail in or out. Gibraltar was, and Gibraltar represented, the very edge of the civilized world. Beyond Gibraltar lay the frontier, the trading posts, the empire. When a ship sailed from Gibraltar, heading south down the African coast, the men aboard were leaving the known world and heading into the unknown; they were leaving the safety and comfort and familiarity of civilization and traveling to the frontier and beyond. Beyond civilization, with all its rules and religion and morality, lay uninhibited freedom. And here every man was a bachelor; every man, free from the watchful eye of society, could behave however he pleased.

If you have read of John Newton, you know the story of a man who enjoyed all that the world beyond Gibraltar had to offer him—at least until God did his work of amazing grace. Press-ganged into service aboard a military ship when he was just nineteen, torn from his home and pulled away from all the people who knew and loved him, Newton quickly tossed aside the religious upbringing of his youth, declaring himself an atheist and proudly blaspheming the God he had forsaken. He soon found himself on the crew of a slave-trading ship.[1]

In those days, slavers would run a triangular route, beginning on the west coast of Africa where they would buy slaves from native or European slave catchers who provided the endless stocks of laborers for the insatiable North American market. Having gathered a load of slaves and having stacked them below decks in unimaginable conditions, the sailors would begin the long and dangerous crossing to America. The slaves who survived the journey were quickly sold. The ship would then sail for England where the men would be able to enjoy the proceeds of another successful series of transactions. And then they would do it all again.

Along the way, the slaves were treated barbarically, and Newton, as did so many of the traders, would tear husbands from wives and children from mothers. He would beat and humiliate; he would assault and violate. Beyond Gibraltar, there was no law. Beyond Gibraltar, beyond the watching eyes of friends and family and neighbors and pastors, every man could be who he wanted to be. Without law and without oversight, there was great freedom, and yet, as Newton would testify, there was also great captivity. In all the freedom to sin, he became bound by his sin, enslaved to it.

In those days, morality and accountability were closely tied to visibility. Most people, in an entire lifetime, would travel no further than the next town or village. They lived in close-knit communities where one person always knew what another was up to. Os Guinness remarks, "Those who did right and those who did not do wrong often acted as they did because they knew they were seen by others.... For most people most of the time, their villages or towns were sufficiently cohesive and their relationships sufficiently close that behavior was held in check."[2] When visibility was lost, as with those men who sailed beyond Gibraltar, so too was accountability. And hard on its heels was morality.

In many years of thinking and writing about issues related to digital living, I don't know that I've found a better illustration than this of the challenge we face as we ponder life after the digital explosion. Today, in our digital world, we spend much of our lives beyond Gibraltar, beyond accountability through visibility, able to say and do and look at and enjoy whatever our hearts desire. Yet for all the freedom it brings us, it can also bring us captivity.

This is particularly true when we discuss issues related to the ways in which we communicate. When we look to what is always true about technology, we see that new technologies inevitably bring both risk and opportunity. Nowhere will we see this so clearly as in the area of communication. With the growth in our ability to communicate comes many tough new challenges but also many great new gospel opportunities. As we consider this, we will first look to the growth of these communications technologies, then see the challenges they bring us, and conclude by understanding how we as Christians must use them for God's glory.

The Growth of Communication

This new digital world is a world built on socializing, on communication, and we are finding that social mores are quickly changing so that we declare people we've never met our friends, and many of us develop our deepest relationships through social networks and games. Some of us experience deeper intimacy in relationships with people we have never seen than in people who can look us in the eyes. We meet up online and carry out much of our courtship through digital media. For growing numbers of us, our first glimpse of a future spouse comes through a picture displayed on a website.* We use Facebook to provide updates on everything we do, combining the mundane with the sublime in one long stream of information. We organize ourselves in new ways, going to church online or working together on a volunteer basis as we create the world's largest, most widely read, and, some would claim, most accurate encyclopedia.

Through it all, we communicate. *Communication* is the tie that binds us all together. Communication lies at the heart of all of these great new devices and technologies we are discussing. What is a cell phone, what is e-mail, what is an Internet connection, what are Facebook and Skype and Twitter, if not new ways of communicating with one another?

Let's look to just two of the ways in which our ability to communicate with others has changed in the past few years, two components of the communications revolution—social media and mobility.

▪ The Rise of Social Media

There was a time, and it seems very long ago now, when the Internet experience largely mimicked the experience of old media. When we searched for news, we would find ourselves at the website owned by a major media outlet—the same outlets that owned the newspapers and television

---

*This was true for two of my three sisters.

channels. We would read the news, much like we might read a newspaper, and then log off and go about life. We had professional content producers who put the information on the Net and consumers of that content who read it, just like it had always been in newspapers and magazines.

As the Internet matured, it brought with it a profound shift. Shortly after we entered the new millennium, we began to hear about Web 2.0, the next generation of websites, the next set of must-have features. Suddenly we began to hear of blogs, where amateur reporters and analysts would filter the news and sometimes provide their own take on it. On such sites, readers were invited to interact, to discuss. News and analysis had become democratized; it had become the realm not just of the expert but of the amateur. Now people were receiving news as filtered by Matt Drudge (Drudge Report) and reading politics as analyzed by Markos Moulitsas Zúniga (Daily Kos) or Andrew Sullivan (The Daily Dish).

Suddenly interactivity was everywhere. It was the one feature every user demanded and became the defining characteristic of social media. First popular among the young and tech-savvy, its appeal soon caught on within every group of web users. What we now know as social media websites became all the rage. MySpace, LiveJournal, Blogger, and hundreds of imitators began to create networks of blogs, networks of people, all of whom had something to say about *something*. Twitter popularized the concept of microblogging, tacitly suggesting that anything worth saying had to be said within a limit of 140 characters. Facebook, launched in February 2004, saw a veritable explosion of growth, first among students and eventually among the general population, until its user base exceeded 500 million. Today the fastest growing population on Facebook is middle-aged women. Social media has passed the tipping point and has come of age.

This term *social media* encompasses many forms, each of which furthers some kind of interactive communication. It is a form of horizontal communication, where content is created and commented on by amateurs, by the crowds of users rather than the few professionals. It was not long before social media dominated almost every part of the online experience. It dominated the web in:

- *communication*: blogs (Blogger, Wordpress), microblogging (Twitter, Buzz), social networking (MySpace, Facebook), travel (TripIt), news aggregation (Netvibes)
- *collaboration*: wikis (Wikipedia), social bookmarking (Delicious, Google Reader), social news (Digg, Reddit)

- *multimedia*: photography (Flickr, deviantArt), video (YouTube, Vimeo), livecasting (Justin.tv, Skype), music (Last.fm, Myspace Music)
- *reviews and opinions*: product reviews (Epinions), business reviews (Yelp, Google), community Q&A (Yahoo! Answers, WikiAnswers)
- *entertainment*: virtual worlds (The Sims Online, Second Life)

Christians were drawn to social media as well. Hundreds of thousands of Christian blogs sprang up, influencing the church in powerful ways. One of *Time* magazine's "10 Ideas Changing the World Right Now" in 2009 was New Calvinism, something others have referred to as Young, Restless, Reformed.[3] New Calvinism is a reaction to the church growth movement that became popular late in the twentieth century and is marked by increased emphasis on expositional preaching, biblical faithfulness, and Calvinistic theology. It is a movement that relied heavily on Christian blogs and social media, one that would not have happened without them.

Along with the demand for interactivity came the desire for customization. The user experience had to be customized so that we could build a presence that would reflect our interests and our passions—that would somehow become a part of our very identity. Facebook allows us to see a stream of updates generated only by our friends. MySpace has allowed a generation of teens to customize an online presence that somehow reflects who they are.

The result of social media is that today we communicate more than ever. And as it has given us the ability, it has given us the desire. We find that we like to communicate whatever we're doing in whatever place we happen to be doing it. Before social media, we didn't think to keep a moment-by-moment breakdown of our days and to broadcast this to the world. Before social media, we would not have cared to read it. Yet today many of us update our Facebook status and Twitter streams with near-religious fervor, almost as if we have not actually experienced anything until we've told others about it. As we may experience a vacation through the little LCD screen of a digital camera, we now experience much of life through social media. What we haven't shared with the world seems like it has hardly been experienced at all.

Social media is one of the great communication transformations that has marked the beginning of the twenty-first century. The other is the increase in mobility.

▪ Mobile Me

You can tell a lot about a person by what he carries with him at all times and in all places. You can tell a lot about a culture by what its people carry in pockets or in purses. The eighteenth-century factory owner who carried an early pocket watch, the kind of device that required skill to build and significant means to own, showed that he valued time and precision. His watch told others that he was a busy man who had to control time if he was to be successful. There was a clear connection between busyness and business. Time was money, and the man who could own time could generate more wealth. In that day, clocks were largely huge machines affixed to the front of the town hall or chiming from the bell towers of churches. The owner of a watch, a miniature clock, had a unique capability—he could take his timepiece with him, allowing him to be mobile but still to maintain the precision he so valued. There was a kind of freedom and status associated with owning this device. A century later, of course, watches were in every pocket, and businessmen would have to look elsewhere to find an advantage over the competition. The ideology of the pocket watch—its emphasis on precision and industrial efficiency—had spread to the entire populace.[4]

The pocket watch provides an interesting historical parallel to the mobile phone. Initially a bulky and prohibitively expensive device available only to businessmen, the first cellular phones were hard-wired into cars and stood as an important status symbol among the elite. They were mobile, but only to a point—many people referred to them as "car phones." Advances in miniaturization and mobile technology steadily increased the power and the effectiveness of such phones, eventually allowing them to become untethered from the automobile.

Today mobile phones are very nearly omnipresent. They are in the pockets of the rich and poor, the businessman and the homemaker, the senior citizen and the student. Communications companies are investing vast amounts of money in generating cellular infrastructure across the African continent and in other Third-World nations. A study sponsored by the United Nations estimates that there are currently over 4 billion cell phone subscribers around the globe. As I mentioned already, on a recent trip to the Dominican Republic I was in the slums of Santo Domingo, in the homes of people who lived in one-room shacks with no running water. And yet even in homes like these were cell phones, and our conversations would often be disrupted by the familiar old ring tones. In fact, in many homes there were only two immediate evidences that we were in the twenty-first century: cell phones and televisions.

The widespread acceptance of mobile technology is the kind of phenomenon that will be discussed in the history textbooks of the future (assuming that textbooks survive the digital explosion). It points to the reality that this digital world is a world of communication—constant, pervasive communication. If it is true that we can tell about a culture by what its people carry all the time, then the fact that there is a cell phone in nearly every pocket tells how much we value communication—especially the *mobile* form of communication.

Mobile phones are just one of many new communications technologies. Along with computers and the Internet, they form the backbone of a communications revolution, a communications explosion. Never have we been able to say so much and through so many different media. We still have all the old media—newspapers, magazines, television, radio—but in addition we have all of these new media. We communicate more now than we ever have before. We do it in more ways and through more devices.

As the cellular phone became nearly omnipresent, we found that we could, and wanted to, use it to communicate all the time. The early cell phones had just one feature: they allowed us to talk. They were sold to us as devices for businessmen or devices that would be an important safety measure when away from home. But soon they allowed us to personalize them, to make them an extension of our personalities, through colors and through ring tones. Then they gave us the ability to message one another. Very quickly, texting went from a minor feature to one that every phone needed to do well. Cameras were added, and eventually video cameras too. Internet access completed the feature set, so that now the phone could be an important link to social media. Wherever we are, we can access Facebook, send updates, read blogs; we can be in touch; we can communicate.

Social media and mobility perfectly complement one another, giving us the desire and the ability to communicate at all times, in all places, in all contexts. The phone keeps us connected to our networks wherever we go. At a time when we are increasingly disconnected from *place*, a cell phone seems to represent home. As long as we have a phone, we can find and be found.

▪ The Idolatry of Communication

In this digital world, communication dominates. In 2010, 141 million blogs were active, 1,052,803 books published, 4.5 billion text messages sent, 175 billion letters mailed, 247 billion e-mails received. Communicating with others is all the rage. It is what we do for business, education, entertainment, devotion. While people have always communicated and have probably always wanted to communicate more, what is unique in our time is its sheer dominance. Our ability to communicate is unprecedented in scope, speed, and reach. It is now the dominant paradigm through which we live our lives.

Perhaps, though, amidst all of the chatter we have forgotten that we do not *need* to communicate all the time. Is it possible that constantly communicating with others is *not* always good, that it can result in problems even as it offers us amazing benefits? Remember one of our key insights into technology: a technology wears its benefits on its sleeve—but the drawbacks are buried deep within.

There are always spiritual realities linked to our use of technology. We know that there is often a link between our use of technology and idolatry, that our idols are often good things that want to become ultimate things in our lives. Communication with others is just this sort of good thing, a *very* good thing that can so easily become an ultimate thing—an idol in our hearts.

How can we tell if something has become an idol in our lives? One possible sign of idolatry is when we devote an inordinate amount of time and attention to something, when we feel less than complete without it. It may be something that we look at right before we go to sleep and the first thing we give our attention to when we wake up. It may be the kind of thing that keeps us awake, even in the middle of the night.

A 2010 study by Oxygen Media and Lightspeed Research sampled the habits of 1,605 young adults. The researchers found that one-third of women between the ages of eighteen and thirty-four check Facebook when they first wake up, before they even head to the bathroom; 21 percent check it in the middle of the night; 39 percent of them declare that they are addicted to Facebook.[5] A Pew Research study found, not surprisingly, that cell phone use is nearly ubiquitous today. Three-quarters of teens and 93 percent of adults between ages eighteen and twenty-nine now have a cell phone. Cell phone use has grown substantially among preteens so that 58 percent of twelve-year-olds now own one.[6]

Lisa Merlo is a University of Florida psychiatrist who studies digital addictions—addictions to the Internet and other technologies. She finds that for a growing number of people, the need to be in constant communication is so powerful that they cannot even turn off their cell phones in order to sit through a movie. Their obsession with their phones resembles other forms of addiction. "As with traditional addictions, excessive cell phone use is associated with certain hallmark patterns of behavior, including using something to feel good, building up a tolerance and needing more of it over time to get the same feeling, and going through withdrawal if deprived of it." A recent Japanese study found that children with cell phones tend not to make friendships with children who do not have them.[7] Clearly, cell phones have the potential to become an idol, determining our behavior and creating patterns of addiction in our lives.

What is really happening here? Why do we feel this constant need to communicate with others? What idol are we serving? There are any number of idols we may be serving through the tools of communication technology:

- We may be serving the idol of *productivity*, communicating so that we feel as though we are being productive, constantly answering work-related e-mails or monitoring work-related social media platforms, feeling the need to respond instantly and decisively morning, noon, or night.
- We may be serving the idol of *significance*, finding a sense of value in the number of people who notice us and interact with us. People with an idol of significance will measure their success or popularity by the number of friends they have on Facebook or the number of followers on Twitter. They make popularity something that can be measured and analyzed and feel that their own significance increases as more people pay attention to them and interact with them online.
- It may be that the very *desire for information* is an idol for us, that we feel as if having more information holds the key to living a better life. For these people, more information is inherently better. To live a good life, to ensure that they are living the best life, they need to be gathering more information, making sure they are constantly in the know, on top of the latest and greatest news. Nothing gets by them. They stay connected—constantly in touch—to remain in the know, feeding the idol of information in their hearts.

Now that it has become such a pervasive part of our lives, it may just be that communication itself has become a cultural idol. In most cases it is not using Facebook or our cell phone that is the real idol. Instead, these technologies serve as enablers and enhancers of the greater idol of communication. When our words (written or spoken) serve an idol, they try to distract us from what matters most. They encourage us to focus on quantity over quality. Our communication begins to lack substance, and the constant flow of words keeps us from focusing our hearts and minds on the truth. The sheer quantity of words can dilute their power and harden our hearts to the Word of God.

But when words serve God, they draw our hearts to the things that are of greatest importance. Such words are full of meaning and life. They call us out of the shallows and into the depths of knowing God. Our technological advances in communication provide us with opportunities to use words in ways that will honor God, thoughtful words that speak with substance and truth and give life to people made in God's image.

We live in an age in which words have become a cheap commodity, and much of our communication has become unbearably light, frustratingly anti-intellectual, and devoid of substance. But words still have power. Used wisely, they can draw people and lead them to what matters most. It is still and always the *Word* that God uses to call his people to himself.

The Challenges of Communication

As we consider the scope of our communication, we come to the unavoidable conclusion that we are making our way into uncharted territory. And whenever we approach a frontier, we need to be especially cautious, unusually careful, as we learn and relearn how to live. This new frontier of constant communication introduces us to difficult challenges and exciting opportunities.

▪ The Decline of Face-to-Face

As we have given ourselves over to online, mediated communication, many have done so at the expense of real-world, face-to-face communication. The same study of young people that compared Facebook habits to bathroom habits found that over half of young women (57 percent) say they spend more time talking to people online than face-to-face. A study from the University of Stanford found that for every hour we spend on our computers, traditional face-to-face interaction falls by nearly thirty minutes. In other words, those two hours you spent on the computer today have likely come at the expense of an hour of face-to-face communication! The four hours you spend tomorrow will come at the expense of two hours of face-to-face contact with those closest to you.

Meanwhile, experience shows that many people now engage online with a depth they cannot sustain when they are offline. Their online relationships are not only more plentiful, but they may also have greater depth than real-world relationships. Studies now show that many young people are actually losing their ability to relate to one another in an offline context. As they've given themselves over to the idol of digital communication, they've paid a price. Now, real-world communication feels threatening, less natural, less normal than typing a text message. It is not unusual to observe two girls sitting in the same room, mere feet from one another, texting back and forth. In some contexts, digital communication has become the more "natural" form of communication. It feels easier, safer, and more efficient than talking face-to-face.

In a strange way, we now find that *more* communication actually leads to *less* communication, or at least less *real-world* communication and less significant communication. Many of our new media technologies are designed for speed and urgency, not for thoughtful reflection and undistracted conversation. They are designed, not to encourage depth in existing relationships, but to widen our network and our ability to say less that is of real substance. Quick and impulsive replies dominate the landscape; thoughtful, longer replies seem out of place and unnecessary.

▪ The Tongue

Exercising restraint in our communication has never been easy, but it is a timeless principle of wisdom.

> When words are many,
> transgression is not lacking,
> but whoever restrains his lips is prudent.
>
> Proverbs 10:19

If such a warning was important in the days of Solomon, how much more is it needed in our day of near-constant communication? We do not need to dip far into the pages of Scripture to learn of the potential blessings and dangers we face in this age of pervasive communication. The Bible bursts with exhortations and commands to guide the way we use our words. It tells us time and again that speech is a *responsibility*. Words can be used to build up or to destroy, encourage or devastate, bring joy or pain.

"Gracious words are like a honeycomb," states Solomon, "sweetness to the soul and health to the body" (Proverbs 16:24). "The tongue of the wise commends knowledge, but the mouths of fools pour out folly" (15:2). "A gentle tongue is a tree of life" (15:4); a righteous tongue is compared to "choice silver" (10:20); a wise and kind tongue is a mark of the excellent wife of Proverbs 31 (31:26). The man who learns to control his tongue, who appreciates its power, will avoid calamity. "Whoever keeps his mouth and his tongue keeps himself out of trouble" (21:23).

But not all people are wise and not all use their tongues in God-honoring ways. One of the seven things God particularly hates is "a lying tongue" (Proverbs 6:17). A "smooth tongue" is used by the adulteress to woo her victims to herself (6:24), and a flattering tongue causes a man to come to dishonor (28:23). In the New Testament, James provides one of Scripture's strongest warnings about our use of words: "How great a forest is set ablaze by such a small fire! And the tongue is a fire, a world of unrighteousness. The tongue is set among our members, staining the whole body, setting on fire the entire course of life, and set on fire by hell" (James 3:5–6).

People tell us that it is a noble and brave thing to speak out whatever words are on our minds at the moment. Outspokenness is considered a virtue, a sign of honesty and authenticity. We are often told that we need to be assertive in saying what we think. Yet the Bible gives us a different word, a word of caution, telling us that our communication must be brought under control and *kept* under control. The first chapter of James tells us that we should be slow to speak. We learn that a person with an unbridled tongue— a person who does not control their communication or think about what they say—is a person whose religion is worthless. The third chapter of James's letter is entirely dedicated to the taming of the tongue, to putting boundaries on our communication so that it can be used for good and not for evil. "With [the tongue] we bless our Lord and Father, and with it we curse people who are made in the likeness of God. From the same mouth come blessing and cursing" (3:9–10). Paul in Colossians exhorts the Christian to make sure that his speech is "gracious, seasoned with salt" (4:6), while in Ephesians, he warns of "corrupting talk," filthy talk that pollutes and destroys instead of blessing and strengthening others (4:29).

God's Word teaches us a key principle that underlies our ability to communicate: *The tongue is connected to the heart.* The words that come out of a person's mouth or are typed on his keypad and texted to a friend are an expression of what is in his heart. When angry words spill out of his mouth, he cannot plead ignorance or circumstance. His words prove that there is an internal corruption. As Jesus said, "What comes out of the mouth proceeds from the heart, and this defiles a person" (Matthew 15:18).

And what of the vast amount of empty, meaningless conversation that goes on today? This must show that there is an emptiness, a lack of substance, in our minds and hearts. Shallow words reveal a shallow heart. Could it be that our digital technologies are encouraging us to live in a world of shallow, meaningless, immediate communication? Are these the ideologies carried within Facebook, within the cell phone? Do they promote significance in communications, or do they seem to prohibit it? Do they promote depth, or breadth?

Perhaps we can summarize the role of the tongue in the life of the Christian with this proverb: "Death and life are in the power of the tongue, and those who love it will eat its fruits" (Proverbs 18:21). Do you see the power of the tongue, the power of words? In his commentary on the passage, Bruce Waltke writes, "The deadly tongue disrupts community and by its lethal power isolates its owner from community and kills him. The life-giving tongue creates community and by its vitality gives its possessor the full enjoyment of the abundant life within the community." Those who understand the tongue, who understand speech "use it fastidiously"; they use it thoughtfully; "they search for chaste expression and precise meaning, and they have an end in view which they will reach because they know what language is for and how it can best be used to achieve its purpose." This purpose may be good, bringing life, or it may be bad, bringing death.[8]

Charles Bridges warns that "no utterance of our tongue can be called trifling. A word, though light as air, may rise up as witness at the throne of judgment for death or for eternal life.... Are not the sins of the tongue an overwhelming manifestation of God's patience? In the inner man the heart is the main thing to guard, in the outer man the tongue."[9] The tongue has the power to shape beliefs, to shape convictions that will affect eternal destinies. Bridges's prayer about the tongue and the heart is one we would all do well to pray. "*Oh, my God, take them both into your own keeping, under your own discipline, as instruments for your service and glory.*"[10]

As the tongue has the power of life and death, it also has the power to heal and destroy. Not only that, but the very same ability that allows us to heal others with a word is the ability that can destroy them. The old adage "sticks and stones may break my bones, but names will never hurt me" is nonsense. "What is done *to* you is of little account besides what is done *in* you."[11] Words are powerful. In fact, it was words that brought the universe into being, and it is the Word who now brings life to the dead heart. Words accomplish; words carry weight; words have meaning; words lift up and words beat down. They bring life and they bring death.

According to the Bible, a controlled tongue is a particular characteristic of the wise, while an out-of-control tongue is a particular mark of the fool. No wonder, then, that among the qualifications of a church leader must be self-control, gentleness, and a desire to avoid quarrels (1 Timothy 3:2–3). In his speech, in his words, in all he says, he must be above reproach. Words are too powerful to use lightly, too important to waste.

With all that the Bible says about the tongue, about our ability to form words, we know that great caution is in order whenever we open our mouths (or begin to type on a keyboard, as the case may be). The caution that marks our speech must also mark our texting, our e-mailing, our commenting, our blogging, and our tweeting. The fact that we communicate at all should cause us to stop and to consider every word. The fact that we communicate so often today and do so before so great an audience should cause us to tremble. As we communicate all day, we give ourselves unending opportunities to sin with our words. Let us end this section where we began:

> When words are many,
>   transgression is not lacking,
>   but whoever restrains his lips is prudent.
>
> Proverbs 10:19

Speaking, Truthing, Loving

There is risk in all of this communication—the risk of misusing our words, of communicating badly. But just as there is risk, there is also a world of opportunity. Just as our words can be used for great evil, they can also be used for great good. In all of the warnings about the words we speak, nowhere are we told to cease speaking altogether. Rather, the Bible puts limits on our speech; it surrounds it with wisdom, with godly character. If we wish to use these new means of communication in ways that honor God and further his work and bring him glory, we must heed what the Bible says to us. We will need to use words wisely.

In Ephesians 4:15, Paul writes, "Speaking the truth in love, we are to grow up in every way into him who is the head, into Christ ..." This passage presents us with three things to focus on as Christians—three ways we must honor God through our ability to communicate: speaking, speaking truth, and speaking truth in love. Let's look to the specific challenges that come to us as we attempt to speak truth in love, to learn the importance of doing so despite the challenges, and to get some practical pointers on how we can do this.

▪ Speaking

This book would serve no purpose if we did not have voices—voices that extend through our fingers, down into our keyboards, across the wires or airwaves, and into the lives of other people. All of these new technologies we discuss—these new devices, these new social media—they are all amazing new ways of extending the tongue. Therefore, what Scripture says is true of words rolling off the tongue is true of words rolling off the keyboard. In either case, the words are an expression of the heart.

We have seen that speaking presents us with a great danger in that words can bring death and life; they can encourage and destroy. If this is true, then great caution is in order. And yet we must still speak. God's words are not meant to frighten us into silence. It would be as great a sin not to speak as to speak rashly, for the God who commands us to speak measured words is the God who commands us that we *must* speak. And he has opened to us these remarkable new opportunities to do that. Just as more people than ever are speaking, more people than ever are listening.

Through all the communication, we as Christians must keep one thing in mind: We have more reason to speak than anyone else. More than believers in any other god, more than adherents to any other faith, we have reason to speak. We speak because God has spoken. Think of the way Scripture belittles the gods of other nations—stumps of wood and chunks of rock that have mouths carved or painted on them. These are gods you may be able to see but ones that have never spoken. Yet we serve a God who *has* spoken and who has spoken *clearly*. His words brought the world into being; his words bring life to the hardened heart; his words bless and sustain us; his words are powerful; his words command us not to be silent but to speak. And so we speak of who he is and of what he has done. We speak what God has spoken and *because* he has spoken. We are to be the speaking followers of the speaking God.[12]

Just as God powerfully used the medium of the written word, the medium of the printing press, and the medium of the radio, he will use these new electronic media. And so, too, will Satan, who will seek to use them to corrupt and destroy. The challenge for the Christian is to learn to use these media with all the opportunities they bring to speak and to tell of this God who speaks through us. We need to use our words to speak his words.

▪ Truthing

Now that we have spoken of speaking, let's look at the truth about truthing. The word *truthing* is a strange one, I know—you won't find it in the dictionary. I use it because it is a helpful word for our purposes as we think about speaking truth in love. It fits the context of this passage, too, since in the original language that this phrase is drawn from, the word *speaking* is absent—it is a logical addition by translators, but one that may obscure the meaning a bit. Really, the text says something like "truthing in love." It is not the speaking we are to emphasize, but the truthing—the telling forth of truth, whether from the pulpit or through the keyboard. And it goes further than that, into the understanding and living and maintaining of that truth. In other words, speaking truth in love, or tweeting truth in love, or blogging or texting or podcasting it—these will all depend on a life that is submitted to the One who is Truth. The message of Ephesians 4:15 is that in all the ways we communicate, we are to truth in love.

We know that we are to speak because God speaks. This is a remarkable privilege and responsibility—one that applies to all who follow Christ. There are times that we must speak truth to unbelievers, but here, in Ephesians 4, Paul is governing the speech between Christians.

Why is it that we are called to speak truth to one another? This is not just the task of teachers and preachers, but the task of any and every Christian. What's the point of it all? The purpose of all this truth is to mature and strengthen one another. "Speaking the truth in love," writes Paul, "we are to grow up in every way into him who is the head, into Christ, from whom the whole body, joined and held together by every joint with which it is equipped, when each part is working properly, makes the body grow so that it builds itself up in love" (4:15–16). By speaking truth to one another we cause the body to grow and as this body grows it builds itself up in love. It displays the love of Christ, the character of Christ, and brings glory to God. What a privilege that we can be part of something so amazing—a body that when working in unity glorifies God! What a motive! What a blessing!

▪ Loving

In our speaking and in our truthing, we must be loving. We see that how we speak the truth is as important as the mere fact that we do it. And we see that we cannot have one without the other. John Stott reminds us:

> Truth becomes hard if it is not softened by love; love becomes soft if it is not strengthened by truth. The apostle calls us to hold the two together,

which should not be difficult for Spirit-filled believers, since the Holy Spirit is himself "the spirit of truth," and his firstfruit is "love." There is no other route than this to a fully mature Christian unity.[13]

And here Stott sets truth and love in their most natural context—that of Christian maturity. It is through maturity in Christ that we learn to speak in a way that honors him. A person who spouts off, a person who has an uncontrollable tongue, a person who has no ability to keep his words in check, this is a person who is immature in the faith.

Paul's exhortation that we are to speak truth in love is written as a means of governing the relationship of one Christian to another. He tells Christians to speak gently, peaceably, and truthfully. The ability to speak truth in love is an ability that comes with increased spiritual maturity. And if this is the case, then one of the greatest threats to biblical unity, one of the threats to true love between believers, is a lack of spiritual maturity.

If we are to be people who speak truth in love, we must be Christians who are growing up, who are striving for maturity. If we are to bring glory to God through all these amazing new platforms God has given to us, if we want to encourage and strengthen one another through them, if we want to display God's love to the world in our display of love to one another, we will need to pursue a mature faith. Such maturity becomes especially important when we live beyond Gibraltar, beyond the eyes of those who keep watch over our souls. We have passwords on our phones and Facebook accounts, and we e-mail anonymously. We have unending opportunities to communicate secretly. It is the wisdom of maturity that will guard us in such times, that will hold our words in check, even when we know no one is looking.

Truth must be the dominant message of our communication, and love must be its prime characteristic. In all the ways God has given us to communicate, we must speak truth, and speak it in love.

To Whom Much Is Given ...

If we as Christians are going to speak truth to one another, we must first be students of truth. The metaphor of the race, used throughout the New Testament, is helpful to consider. An athlete does not plod his way through a race, but he pushes himself, fighting for position, pushing his body to its limits and maybe just a bit beyond. As students of the truth, we must push ourselves to learn more, to know more, to come to a greater and greater understanding of the character of God.

But even as we are students of truth, we must also be students of love. As followers of Christ, we have before us the perfect example of love. We have been saved by an act of love so great that eternity will still not provide enough time for us to exhaust our words as we plumb the depths of Christ's great sacrifice. This is the love Frederick Lehman wrote about in his great hymn "The Love of God." In the final stanza he writes:

> Could we with ink the ocean fill,
> And were the skies of parchment made,
> Were every stalk on earth a quill,
> And every man a scribe by trade,
> To write the love of God above
> Would drain the ocean dry.
> Nor could the scroll contain the whole,
> Though stretched from sky to sky.

Today he might forgo the parchment and quills to remind us that even if every man were to e-mail and blog and text for all of time, we would never tire of communicating about this amazing love. A trillion text messages a year would only scratch the surface.

> O love of God, how rich and pure!
> How measureless and strong!
> It shall for evermore endure
> The saints' and angels' song.[14]

To whom much is given, much is required. Today, living at the dawn of this century, we have amazing new opportunities to communicate truth and love. We have amazing new opportunities to do this as the community of God's people, joined together in this body whose head is Christ. We are joined together to bring special glory to God, if we can learn to speak the truth—and to speak it in love. Today we can do this across the world in an instant, to thousands of brothers and sisters whom we may never meet on this side of eternity. What an opportunity! What a blessing!

Paul writes, "Let all that you do be done in love" (1 Corinthians 16:14). In all your speaking, in all your truthing, let love guide. Let love sustain. For God's sake, speak. Speak truth. Speak truth in love.

Christian Communication

In the introduction, I referred to the three circles of experience, theory, and theology and promised that we would seek to find ways to live in the sweet spot between them. Now that we have learned about the new challenges of communication in a digital world, let's see how we can communicate well. Let's see how each of us can hold theology, theory, and experience together, regarding them as essential components of Christian communication in a digital world.

Each of us has a lot of *experience* with digital communications. Every time we send an e-mail, read a blog, talk on a cell phone, or watch a DVD, we are sending or receiving some kind of communication. Experience shows us how much we love to do this, how much this kind of communication has become an integral component of our culture. We assume that our friends are on Facebook, that they have an e-mail address, that they carry a cell phone with them at all times. The few who do not are the exception to the rule. Experience is also showing that there are new realities to grapple with—the difficulty of communicating well all the time, the ease with which we can misuse these great gifts.

Our *theory* of technology tells us that there are always unexpected consequences to our use of it, that with all of the benefits come inevitable drawbacks. And we know that we must be diligent in seeing the drawbacks that tend to be hidden from our view.

Our *theology* of technology tells us that while our new devices do not have any innate morality—they are neither good nor evil—they inhabit a sinful world and will draw our hearts away from God more easily than toward him. We know that though our devices are not sinful, we may well use them in sinful ways. In all the ways we communicate today, we may use our technologies to destroy relationship instead of foster it, to tear down instead of build up. If we are to use them well, we must use them deliberately, thoughtfully, and in a distinctly Christian way. On the other hand, if we live outside the sweet spot, we may be unaware of the power of our words. We may neglect to speak truth or to make love central in all we speak and write.

Through the Bible God calls us to speak truth in love. Truth and love are the twin pillars that should uphold all of our communication. And in this age of pervasive communication they are as important as ever. How can we ensure in practical ways that we are speaking truth in love? Some small measures can do wonders.

Be visible. If anonymity can be an enemy and a refuge, then visibility can work to keep us from slipping into sinful patterns of living and communicating. Simply by removing the anonymity of the web we can guard our hearts. When you find yourself pursuing anonymity, question your heart. You may well find that you are doing so for the worst of motives. Live a visible life, even as you use gadgets and technologies that almost beg to be kept private. Remember, "The eyes of the LORD are in every place, keeping watch on the evil and the good" (Proverbs 15:3), and, "Nothing is hidden that will not be made manifest, nor is anything secret that will not be known and come to light" (Luke 8:17).

Be accountable. Do not live your online life apart from accountability and oversight. Let friends or family know what you are doing online; invite them into your digital world. Have someone keep up with your blog or check in on your Facebook status. This will go a long way to ensuring that you think twice before hitting the Post button, and it will give him free rein to approach you with words of warning or caution or rebuke when necessary.

Be real. Don't fabricate for yourself an identity online that is vastly different from your real-world identity. There is so much temptation to be someone you are not when you are online, but this can prove to be just the start of a drift into an increasingly fantastical presentation of yourself. Be the person that God has made you to be, even in the online world. And as you commit to being yourself, focus on quality communication, being willing to say less in order to say more.

Be mature. To sum it up, you will need to act like a mature Christian. Paul draws a clear connection between maturity and the ability to speak truth in love. While maturity is not easy, and it requires labor, there is no great trick to it. We simply commit ourselves to those things that God tells us to do, while turning away from those things he tells us to avoid. We join in community with other Christians where we can live our lives visibly before them, eager and thankful for their guidance and, if necessary, their rebuke. We commit to studying Scripture and communing with God in prayer. We use the gifts God has given us to serve one another. And we relentlessly pursue the truth, learning what is true and how to integrate that truth into our lives.

Be visible; be accountable; be real; be mature. And always distrust yourself. It may sound harsh, but be willing to doubt your motives, your heart. Take a moment to pray before answering an antagonistic e-mail; bounce your ideas and articles off trusted friends before posting them; be slow to speak (or type) and quick to listen.

QUESTIONS FOR REFLECTION

1. How much of your digital life is lived visibly, before the eyes of a friend, a spouse, a parent, a pastor? Do you find that you tend toward visibility or anonymity?

2. What kinds of boundaries or limits have you placed on your communication? Have you found it challenging to communicate only at certain times or in certain places or contexts? Or are you in near-constant communication through your devices? It may be interesting to ask your spouse, your parents, or your friends what they think about your habits.

3. Today we communicate more often than ever before, but in such a way that much of our communication is low in quality and low in content. How have you found this to be true in your life? In what situations is it especially tempting for you to replace quality with quantity?

4. What are some contexts in which you may need to communicate less in order to communicate better? What are some ways you communicate that seem to prohibit significant, meaningful conversation?

5. Amid all of the communication we are doing today, what are some ways we can intentionally use words in ways that really matter?

CHAPTER 5

LIFE in the REAL WORLD (Mediation/ Identity)

Where were you on September 11, 2001? Do you remember what you were doing when you first heard that an airplane had hit the World Trade Center? Can you recall who you were with when you suddenly realized that America was under attack? You doubtlessly remember many of the details—who you were with, what you were doing, where you went that day. You remember them because there is a sense in which you lived through the attack—experiencing the events of that day by watching it unfold on a screen before you, participating in what was happening through the medium of the television or the Internet. You saw the buildings burn *as they were burning*; you saw them tremble and collapse; and you heard the panicked screams of terrified New Yorkers as they ran away from the falling towers. You saw it as it happened.

Rewind to December 7, 1941, and again, we see America under attack. But if you were to ask your grandparents where they were on December 7, 1941, what they were doing at that moment when they heard that the Japanese had launched a surprise attack on Pearl Harbor, and what they did when they found out—you might be surprised at their response. Most people of that generation *won't* remember what they were doing or how they reacted, and not because more time has passed since the events of that day. They won't remember the events of that day because *they did not live through them in the same way.* They were not able to watch the attack unfold on the television screen. They did not experience firsthand the destruction and the immediate pain of loss and death. Instead, they waited for newspaper reports and telegrams to provide details as they emerged over hours, days, and weeks.

In some ways there are great similarities between the attacks of 1941 and 2001, and in some ways they could not be more different. Though just sixty years had elapsed, the world had changed. Our digital, televised world allowed us all to live through the events of 9/11 in a vicarious way, to actually bring us close to the scene of the disaster. Our mediated world allowed us to participate in the event in a way that was not possible just six decades before. In the six decades between attacks, we had transitioned from having no screens in our homes, in our lives, to living in their constant presence. Just as people remembered where they were when President John F. Kennedy was shot and how they immediately rushed to a television screen, a new generation can vividly remember where they were on September 11 thanks to the mediated experience of digital technology.

Our lives have become saturated with sounds and images flashing in front of our eyes, blaring into our ears. Sociologist and author Todd Gitlin states rightly, "Life experience has become an experience in the presence of media."[1] At work we spend forty hours staring at computer screens. At home we watch television or visit our favorite websites. Between work and home we check our route on the GPS and dash off a few text messages.* Even at church we watch our pastors on screens before returning home to watch sermons on the Internet. Life is mediated by the screen.

Just how much are screens an essential part of life in the twenty-first century? In 2008, the Council for Research Excellence decided to find out.[2] They worked with Nielsen to carry out a broad research project that would monitor media usage for 476 Americans. Using a small data-collecting device running specialized software, an observer monitored each of the subjects for two full waking days, yielding a total of three-quarters of a million minutes of observation time measured in ten-second increments.

---

*Not a great idea, by the way. I recently saw a church sign that read, "Honk if you love Jesus. Text while driving if you want to meet him."

Here are a few of the more significant results of their study:

- Adults ages forty-five to fifty-four accumulate the greatest amount of screen time, totaling nine hours and thirty-four minutes per day. The average daily screen time for eighteen-year-olds is slightly less at eight and a half hours. Screen time for those under eighteen lacks thorough studies at the moment but is thought to be at least equal to that of eighteen-year-olds.
- About a quarter of that screen time is "combined time," meaning that during these periods people are using more than one screen at once — perhaps watching TV while surfing the Internet, or watching a movie while texting and checking e-mail. The *accumulated* screen time is about two hours more than the *actual* screen time.
- Time in front of the television screen, whether watching television, watching a DVD or playing a console game, still makes up the largest amount of time — about five hours for the eighteen-year-old and a bit more for Mom and Dad. It rises very sharply as Mom and Dad become Grandma and Grandpa. Those who are age sixty-five and older average well over seven hours per day of TV time.
- When we analyze these screen times, we realize that the average American spends approximately one hour per day watching television commercials and other promos.

In 1946, only one half of 1 percent of American households had even a single screen in their home. Just over six decades later, virtually every home has a multitude of screens, and we are spending at least eight and a half hours every day in front of them. With the current pace of change, even this study, conducted in 2008, is already dated. More and more of life is lived in the presence of media. It goes without saying that such a profound change carries with it significant consequences for our families, for the culture, and for the church.

In this chapter, we are going to look at the rise of media in our lives through the theme of *mediation*, seeking to understand what it means that we now live so much of our life *through* the screen. Why are we so drawn to screens and visual images? And what effect is all of this having on our lives? On our hearts?

What Is Media?

If you read five books on media, you will find five different definitions for the terms *media* or *medium*. They range from Marshall McLuhan's all-encompassing statement that a medium is anything that extends or amplifies a human capacity (in which case a microphone is a medium that extends the voice, and a hammer is a medium that extends the hand) to definitions that are far too narrow to be useful. So let me propose a simple and straightforward definition: *A medium is, quite simply, something that stands between.* Mathematically, it refers to the number that stands in the middle of an ordered list, halfway between the beginning and the end. In spiritualism, it refers to a person who acts as an intermediary between the living and the dead. It is at the root of the word *mediator,* a role we find described in the Scriptures. In the Old Testament, Moses served as the mediator between God and Israel, his people. Moses represented the people to God, and God to the people. And in his mediatorial role, Moses pointed forward to Christ, the full and final mediator between God and man (1 Timothy 2:5).

What, then, does it mean to talk about mediation in reference to our communication via digital technology? A digital medium is a device or tool or technology that delivers some kind of data or information. *It stands between the one who creates sounds or images and the one who receives them.* In concrete terms, whenever we speak of these "digital media," we are really just talking about our computers and iPods and e-readers and cell phones and all those electronic devices that have some kind of a screen that allows us to communicate visually. Through these devices we receive sounds and images and words. Through these devices we live much of our lives.

Never before in human history have people lived their lives so thoroughly and consistently mediated as we do today. A generation before us may have watched television, but television was never an all-encompassing media, despite the fears of critics in the 1970s and 80s. And while television has dominated our leisure time for the past few decades, it was never able to make significant inroads in the workplace, the classroom, and the sanctuary. With the rise of the screen, now attached to other digital technologies, we are suddenly approaching a turning point in human experience. Soon we will be spending more time in the glare of a screen than we spend outside of it. Screens are present in class, in church, at work, at play, and at leisure. They are mounted in the seats in front of us on airplanes, and they hang from the ceilings of our vans and SUVs. Screens are on our desks and in our pockets, rarely more than a few feet away.

Face-to-Face

Is all this necessarily bad? Is there anything wrong with communicating through these media, with living a mediated life with minimal face-to-face contact? While there may be some unique opportunities afforded by mediated contact, I would argue that it is, in fact, a lower form of communication, one that is intended to be a mere supplement to our lives. The best relationships we can have are *not* those that rely on mediation, but rather the ones that allow for *unmediated* contact and communication. This becomes apparent as we examine God's intention for us as people made in his image. What type of relational interaction were we made for, and why is a mediator now necessary for us to experience relational intimacy? The Bible does, in fact, teach us that mediation is necessary for us to know God and fully love one another, but as we will see, this mediated communication is a concession from God and a consequence of man's sin. Face-to-face contact between human beings is inherently richer and better than any mediated contact.

▪ The Im-mediate God

There are some English words whose meaning we understand without difficulty and some that seem to require a little more work. When we think of the word *immature*, we understand that the prefix *im-* means *not*. A person who is immature is someone who is *not* mature — he displays a lack of maturity. But a similar word, *immediate*, may not strike us in quite the same way. If we break off the prefix, we find the word *mediate*. The word *im-mediate* harkens back to an older and less common understanding of the word. *The American Heritage Dictionary* defines *immediate* as "acting or occurring without the interposition of another agency or object; direct." In other words, *immediate* indicates access that requires *no* mediation. It describes the type of relational communication that man enjoyed with God before the appearance of sin — direct and face-to-face.

Have you ever considered what it must have been like for Adam and Eve to walk and talk with God in the garden of Eden? Have you thought of the things you might say to God, the things you might ask him, if you were to hear his footsteps today? What Christian hasn't experienced a pang of jealousy when he reads, "They heard the sound of the LORD God walking in the garden in the cool of the day" (Genesis 3:8)? And what Christian hasn't experienced a pang of remorse when he reads about Adam and Eve squandering that unique privilege?

After disobeying God's command and eating the fruit of the forbidden tree, Adam and Eve once again heard God walking in the garden as he had done in the past. This time, as Adam and Eve recognized the sound of his footsteps, instead of rushing to him and rejoicing in his presence, they fled and hid in fear and shame. They had sinned and knew there would be consequences for their disobedience. For the very first time, they feared their Maker. In order for them to be in his presence, God would have to *mediate* himself to them. The face-to-face intimacy they had enjoyed was lost.

Ever since this fall into sin, the history of God's people has been a history of experiencing God through mediation. By rejecting God's goodness and putting himself in place of God, Adam erected a barrier between himself and his Maker. The close communion that had once existed was ruptured and destroyed. No longer would God come walking to them in the cool of the day. No longer could he allow them to stay in his garden. Adam and Eve were forced out and the way was barred so they could not return. The direct line of communication was disconnected.

All mediation involves overcoming some kind of limitation. Spiritual mediation involves overcoming a relational limitation, one that takes account of our sin and God's holiness. From the moment of Adam's first sin, God could no longer allow people to commune with him in the same way they had before. His holy character could not allow for the presence of such unholy, sinful beings. From that point forward, God's people could no longer approach him as they had in the garden. They now had to approach him through mediators like Moses. After Moses came Joshua and countless judges and prophets to lead the people. God raised up priests who were responsible for standing between God and man, offering sacrifices on behalf of the people and bestowing blessings and curses on behalf of God. The people understood that sin was the cause of their inability to approach God as they were. They must have inevitably wondered, *How can we approach God directly?* The presence of mediators stirred in them a longing for something better.

We are created with an innate desire for *unmediated* contact and communication with God. Though sin has disrupted this contact, requiring a mediator between God and man, God promises that in the full and final redemption, in the new heaven and the new earth, we will once more experience him in the direct and unmediated way we were created for. This unmediated contact is seen in the promise of 1 Corinthians 13, that great chapter on the fulfillment of love, where Paul writes, "For now we see in a mirror dimly, but then face to face. Now I know in part; then I shall know fully, even as I have been fully known" (1 Corinthians 13:12). It is found in the promise of Revelation 22:4, where we read that God's servants "will see his face," and in the promise of 1 John 3:2, which states, "Beloved, we are God's children now, and what we will be has not yet appeared; but we know that when he appears we will be like him, because we shall see him as he is." It is this face-to-face contact with Christ, this final intimacy with God himself, that has sustained the hope of generations of Christians.

R. C. Sproul writes:

> The final goal of every Christian is to be allowed to see what was denied to Moses. We want to see Him face-to-face. We want to bask in the radiant glory of His divine countenance. It was the hope of every Jew, a hope instilled in the most famous and beloved benediction of Israel: "The LORD bless you and keep you; the LORD make his face shine upon you and be gracious to you; the LORD turn his face toward you and give you peace" (Numbers 6:24–26).[3]

While mediation is a necessity in this sinful world, it is a *concession*. We are grateful that God gives us the Son and the Holy Spirit as mediators so we can pray to him, worship him, and receive his blessings. But we still long for that broken fellowship to be fully restored. In this life, while mediation is good, we know that the spiritual intimacy we long for—the direct presence of God—will be so much better.

▪ The Im-mediate Man

If the ideal means of communication between God and man is unmediated, so too is the ideal communication between humans. We write letters to those we cannot be near to, but always we long to be with them. We send e-mails and text messages when we have to, but we know that it is best to *be with* the people we love, to be in their presence, to be able to see them face-to-face. No young man, smitten with fond affection for a girl, stands beside her and says, "I long to write letters to you." No, he writes her letters and says, "I long to *be with* you!"

All of our communication technologies seek to overcome some kind of limitation. Our voices are not loud enough to carry from one end of the nation to another, so we use e-mail and phone calls to communicate with friends and family members who live far away. These are great abilities, but they do not come without a cost. As our information technologies extend one or more of our abilities, they also tend to *disembody* the information they convey. While they enhance one ability, they diminish another.

This has always been true with communication technology. For example, consider the transition from an oral culture to a written culture, the time when humans first learned to record words in writing: "What once required memorization and recitation by living persons could now be retrieved through the dead pages of papyri, parchment, or paper."[4] Pause for just a moment to consider the implications of this shift. There was a time when people who wanted to encounter the words of God would need to rely on the expertise of an oral poet, a person whose task it was to memorize and recite the Scriptures. But when humans transitioned to a written culture (and eventually a print culture), suddenly every person could read the Bible on his own, and the poet became superfluous, unnecessary. The change in media brought about a vast shift—not only by giving more people an opportunity to encounter more of God's words, but in the very way that people understood the purpose and meaning of these words. The poet disappeared. And so did all of the ideas and ways of interpreting that were part and parcel of communication via the spoken word. It cost us a certain element of richness, a depth that is available in face-to-face, immediate conversation.

Today, as we increasingly use e-mail or text messaging as replacements for face-to-face communication, we no longer have access to the signals of voice and body language that are an integral part of oral communication. We have discovered that without these signals it is far more difficult to communicate clearly, especially when trying to communicate our emotions. This is why people have invented "emoticons"—little icons made up of a series of characters that provide the cues that formerly came through tone and unspoken gesture. The ability to communicate further and overcome the limitation of distance has come at the price of real presence: "The voice extends and the person recedes."[5]

Writing specifically about e-mail, John Freeman says,

> The truth is that text rarely, if ever, can equal the richness of a face-to-face conversation. It's static, disembodied. It does not convey hand gestures, verbal tone, inflection, or facial expressions, things we are taught from birth to encode and decode. Indeed, these are some of the first things children learn when speaking; even before they can form words, they mimic the cadences and tones of speech they have heard. They gesture. We learn to communicate with our bodies. Talk on the phone with a friend across the globe, and you will discover how hard a habit this is to break. There are your hands, waving and punctuating, even though your friend cannot see them. It's hardwired into us. Even the blind talk with their hands.

And this is just the body. Text, until this point, has also had a kind of body: the page. Formal letters came on heavy paper stock; notes dashed off while traveling came on the stationery of hotels; postcards forced correspondents to become prose poets to close the gap between what was on the card and what they were writing; telegrams with a black rim were to be dreaded. Electronic messages are completely devoid of this sensuality; they all arrive in the same format. They have no messenger bringing them there, as an interpreter. As a result, the tone of e-mails is misunderstood more than half of the time, compared to just a quarter of the time over the phone and even less often face-to-face.[6]

Clearly, mediated communication is quite different from immediate communication. Because it involves less of us, it offers less and delivers less. When I am face-to-face, I communicate through my voice, through gesture, through tone, through body language, through a shifting of the eyes or a nervous tic. When I communicate in a mediated way, these social cues begin to disappear until, when I send an e-mail or a text message, they disappear almost entirely. As we become more reliant on digital forms of communication, we tend to become more one-dimensional in our relationships with others.

While it is true that people are finding creative ways of overcoming some of these limitations, it remains clear that face-to-face communication is far superior to any kind of mediated communication. To put it another way, electronic, disembodied communication can be one of the worst ways of communicating. This is particularly true as we move toward technologies that offer less of us rather than more (which is to say that text messaging is worse than video chat). To be clear, this is not to say that virtual communication has no place or that e-mail is necessarily sinful. Like any technology, the ability to communicate through media has certain benefits, and for these we give thanks to God. But as we have seen, every technology inhabits this sinful world and will naturally seek to enhance our idols and increase the power of sin over us. At its best, digital communication can be a *supplement* for real communication, but whenever possible should be a *minor* component to the many ways we can interact with one another. It is certainly not a suitable replacement for face-to-face contact.

And yet here we find ourselves living in a mediated world. Mediated communication is often a choice we make. Many people today prefer to dash off an e-mail rather than drive across town or walk next door. Many young people send text messages, even to people sitting in the same room.

I spoke to some friends recently, a husband and wife who are in the habit of chatting on instant messenger when she is in one room and he is in the next. Why would we choose such mediated contact, particularly when we can experience face-to-face communication? What is its allure?

Of course, there are many good reasons to be grateful for mediated communication. I have spoken to people with disabilities whose lives have been transformed by their digital devices. I have seen businesses and ministries grow and thrive because of the efficiency, the speed, and the abilities enhanced by digital communications. We do well to be thankful for mediated communication and for its many benefits. Yet we do need to ensure that in all the ways we communicate we move toward *true intimacy* and avoid distancing ourselves from one another.

Let's be grateful that God has not turned his back on us once and for all but has given us Jesus Christ and the Holy Spirit—that through the Spirit and because of the work of Christ we can once more come boldly before him. And yet let's always long for the day when we will be perfected, when once more we can come into the presence of this holy God and know even as we are known. Yes, let's be grateful for the mediation that allows us to communicate with one another, whether through the medium of the book you are reading right now or the e-mail you will send later on. And yet let's remember that it is real face-to-face contact that is best, that communicates most, and that builds true friendship, true intimacy.

Digital Disincarnation

Our digital technologies "stand between" in order to extend our ability to communicate, to allow us to communicate constantly and through a wide variety of media. As we do this, we extend ourselves beyond ourselves; we extend our mediated presence beyond our physical presence. We have always been able to do this to a degree—we have been able to extend our voices through letters or postcards to friends. And yet we always knew that what we were sending through the mail was not *us* but simply a representation of our words. But as we increasingly migrate to the digital world, we find ourselves wrestling with new issues related to our identity, with how our digital presence relates to who we really are.

Let's look to the movies for a metaphor. The film *Avatar* premiered in London in December 2009 and opened a week later to rave reviews. It smashed a long list of box office records and quickly became the highest-grossing film of all-time, surpassing such blockbusters as *Titanic* and *The Lord of the Rings: The Return of the King*. The protagonist in this science-fiction story is Jake Sully, a Marine who has paraplegia. Sully is brought to the planet of Pandora to carry out an important mission. Living on Pandora are the Na'Vi, a race of ten-foot-tall, blue-skinned humanoid creatures who live in complete harmony with one another and with nature. They worship Eywa, the "All Mother," the goddess of nature. Sully is tasked with infiltrating this people and learning about their culture and ultimately finding a way to defeat them so humans can exploit the bounties of their world. To do this, he must operate an avatar, a virtual body.

In 2007, long before the movie's release, a reporter for *Time* magazine asked its creator, James Cameron, what an avatar is. Cameron replied, "It's an incarnation of one of the Hindu gods taking a flesh form. In this film what that means is that the human technology in the future is capable of injecting a human's intelligence into a remotely located body, a biological body."[7]

Using a machine, Jake Sully creates a mental link with a Na'Vi body. While his real body, damaged and crippled, lies within a machine, he is able to move his consciousness into the living and active body of a Na'Vi. And it is through this body, this avatar, that he explores the world of Pandora. It is through this body that he lives the kind of life he could only have dreamed of while still being within his "real" body, his paraplegic body. As a Na'Vi, he is stronger and faster, whole and complete; he can run and jump and fly. He is a whole new man.

Sully's existence on Pandora is a mediated one, one in which his body is in one location and his consciousness is in another. He is able to be physically present in one place and yet still mentally and spiritually present in another. He experiences Pandora through his avatar.

Jake Sully lived a life that was mediated by his avatar. He saw the world through its eyes, experienced it through its hands, tasted it through its tongue. And like Sully, we increasingly find ourselves living through our media today, through our devices, through our screens. So much of what we experience from day to day comes into our eyes and ears through some form of digital technology. We relate to one another through Facebook, talk to one another through webcams, date one another through instant messengers, read books through our e-readers, live our vacations through the little screens on our digital cameras. It seems that every experience of life can now be carried by digital media.

And like Sully, we can begin to *identify* with our media and feel more comfortable within them than outside of them. As we grow closer and closer to our media and become more dependent on them, as we experience more of life through them, we begin to make our mediated selves a part of our identity. We extend ourselves from flesh-and-blood churches to virtual churches or from classrooms at the local university to virtual classrooms in an online learning school. We play massively multiplayer video games and find that we prefer the online, virtual representations of ourselves to the people we are in the real world. Some of us step into virtual worlds, where we take on avatars of our own. They are not as advanced or complete as the ones envisioned by James Cameron, but they are captivating nonetheless.

And though not all of us have participated in a virtual world where we live through an avatar, still we've seen that who we are online may be very different from who we are in the real world. We have seen that, even though these experiences promise something called *community*, this is a very different kind of community from the one we experience in the home, in the neighborhood, in the local church. We've seen that it is possible to be one person offline and a very different person online. We've seen that there are confusing new issues related to mediated reality.

Through it all, the self threatens to become disconnected, disengaged from the body. We become digitally disincarnated, people who can live and *be* online, present only in a virtual, mediated sense. Increasingly who we are is no longer the person people meet face-to-face, but the mediated identity we have created. At first, we merely extended a sense of self into cyberspace, but eventually it took root there and in some cases now threatens to surpass the real self—the self that includes not just a mind and a soul but a physical presence as well.

Perhaps the heart of this confusion is our insistence that the Internet is a *there*, that it is a place. We never referred to the space between my mailbox and my friend's mailbox as a place (letterspace?). Letters were in transit. They were in trucks or on trains, but they were not in a place. When I wrote a letter, I was not entering a "letter world." Similarly, when I watched TV, an inherently nonparticipatory act, I was still in my living room, not in some strange place between my home and the cable company. But when it comes to the Internet, we talk about entering *cyberspace*, a space that is really no "place" at all. We insist that when we participate in an online forum or take on a character in an Internet-based video game, we are present somewhere and somehow. We take our sense of self, our sense of presence, and transport it into the ethereal world of bits and bytes. Suddenly we are here *and* there, at a desk in body but in soul or spirit somehow present in cyberspace. And this is new to us, new to the human experience. When we venture into this world, this mediated world, we leave our bodies behind. And more and more of us are finding that we actually like it this way, that being able to experience a space free from the limitations of real presence brings a kind of joy.

▪ The New Gnosticism

Let's go back to *Avatar* for just a moment. *Avatar* is, at its heart, a religious film, one that celebrates pantheism, the belief that God is not just present in nature but that God *is* nature. Pantheism calls all human beings to greater unity, greater love, by joining in harmony with the world around us. We will find peace, it assures us, when we embrace nature, embrace the fact that all is One. *Avatar* tells us that the soul is superior to the body, that while the body is necessarily corrupt, polluted by its dependence on matter, the soul is pure. And in this way it calls us back to Gnosticism, a controversial religion that triggered the warning lights of the very earliest Christians.

The heart of Gnosticism is the belief that what is *spiritual* is essentially good, while what is *material*—the physical world we can taste, touch, see, and smell—is essentially bad, corrupted. To put this in technological terms, Gnosticism teaches that humans are in a process of evolution that will eventually take them from hardware to software, from embodiment to an ultimate, and inherently better, state of disembodiment. The ultimate hope of all beings is to overcome the trappings of the flesh, the boundaries of the body, and to return to the One, the god that is in all and that is all. Such a belief is common to many of the world's religions and especially the Eastern religions. It is also commonly found in some of our most popular shared cultural stories—movies such as *Star Wars*, *The Matrix*, *Avatar*, and countless others.

Gnosticism is not a new phenomenon. It has existed in one form or another for thousands of years. It advocates beliefs and teachings that are opposed to the Bible yet are consistent with the kinds of religions humans create when they have turned their backs on the truth.

The first chapter of Romans tells us that sinful human beings willfully suppress the knowledge of God, pushing away knowledge that God has implanted within them, knowledge of God's very existence and character.

This suppression manifests itself in two ways: first through minimizing and ultimately eradicating the Creator-creature distinction, and then by creating an alternative worldview to replace biblical truth. Peter Jones of TruthXchange argues that what fills the vacuum left by abandoning a biblically informed worldview will inevitably tend toward monism, the view that truth can be found within creation rather than outside of it. Worldviews like this insist that what is spirit is superior to what is flesh, that the hope of humanity is to escape the flesh in order to rise to something better and more advanced.

But nothing could be further from the truth. The apostle John speaks in the harshest terms about those who taught that Christ did not come in the medium of the flesh. In coming to earth as a man, Christ showed us the dignity God gives to flesh and blood. And Christ has been raised in a physical body, forever God and forever man—forever God in the body of a man. Hinduism, Buddhism, and Gnosticism all deny the inherent goodness of our bodies. These religions claim to save us *from* the body, not *with* or *in* the body.

These age-old heresies and alternative religious teachings are not far removed from the allure and promise of cyberspace, a "place" where we can experience life in a pure way, a way detached from the constraints of place and physical presence. Cyberspace has given us a new way of understanding the relationship of life and being to our flesh-and-blood bodies. We now see cyberspace as a place but also as a state of being. Cyberspace gives us a place to be ourselves *apart from our bodies*. And in many cases the draw is irresistible. Often, we are led to view this as a superior alternative to the real world. Why? Because it is a place that allows us to break free of the limits of our bodies and our God-given circumstances.

In *The Soul in Cyberspace*, Douglas Groothuis writes of a woman who suffers from a serious social phobia that has left her extremely anxious in social situations and, as a consequence, increasingly isolated and alone.[8] But through the Internet she was able to find others who suffered from a similar condition, and together they have been able to interact and form a kind of community. Here they have found the friendship and fellowship that their conditions have denied them in the real world. Here, in a world without her body and all of its limitations, she has found a place to be herself.

But has this woman truly found freedom from the limitations of her flesh? There is a sense in which she has—she has been able to find a way of overcoming her inability to communicate. And yet, there is another sense in which she has not really found freedom at all because she is still bound by her condition, a condition that keeps her from finding and experiencing community in the real world. She is still a captive to the four walls that keep her from the world of flesh and blood. Cyberspace has provided a sense of community but has also furthered her captivity by giving her the illusion of freedom. That she believes she is now free from this limitation only shows just how captive she remains to its power. She has accepted the promise of Gnosticism—that life without the physical is as good or better than life within it. But this denies what the Bible tells us: "In the biblical teaching, matter is something not to be escaped but redeemed."[9] Freedom without the body, freedom without what makes us whole and complete human beings, is really no freedom at all.

The new, postmodern form of Gnosticism that we see today also promotes a fluidity of identity. Postmodernism tells us that we can be gay then straight, male then female. (Or why not both at once? Or why not neither one?) Online life promises us much the same—we can be one thing and then another or one thing and at the same time another. "Taking on various identities in varying circumstances is sanctioned by this new movement, for it exemplifies the death of belief in the unitary self, the hard ego, the irreducible center of personal identity. Identity is not fixed, but fluid; not singular, but multiple; not prescribed, but protean; not defined, but diffused."[10] What we are in virtual worlds is just an expression of what we believe culturally.

This new Gnosticism calls us to a wholehearted embrace of mediated communication and quietly begins suggesting to our hearts that this way of life may actually be superior. It calls us to disincarnate ourselves, to increasingly replace the world of flesh and blood with an alternate world of bits and bytes. It tells us that we can overcome the limitations imposed on us by simply embracing the virtual, the cyberself. Here in the cyberworld I can be popular. I can be powerful. I can be a somebody. And yet I do it all at the expense of who I really am.

Real Space and Cyberspace

Community was once largely found within a person's geographical context. For many years, it was a necessity that we had to find our relational closeness with those with whom we also shared geographical closeness. But as our technologies have advanced, we have found clever ways of expanding and extending our communities beyond geographic boundaries.

The automobile and the highway have transformed churches so that community churches that once drew from a single neighborhood have now moved to the suburbs and become commuter churches, drawing worshipers from across an entire city. Interstates and airplanes have allowed us to expand communities further still so that what used to be a local show for enthusiasts of a particular hobby can now be international in its scope, drawing together a community from around the world. Such communities brought people together relationally but also physically—we gathered together around a shared interest, but we were still all together in one spot. What is markedly different about our new digital communities is that they bring people together apart from their bodies. We now consider *community* what was previously mere *communication*.

It used to be that a sense of belonging was provided by a household or a community. We were always rooted to a specific context. If you wanted to call me on the phone, you had to call the family telephone; if you wanted to send me a letter, you would post it to the family home. In both cases, I was rooted to a context of geography and a context of relationship. But now, through mobile phones, e-mail, and a thousand other digital technologies, you can communicate with me in a way that is uprooted from a family or geographical context. Consider that Apple now offers e-mail addresses ending with @me.com. Sociology professor Barry Wellman and several other researchers write:

> Because connections are to people and not to places, the technology affords shifting of work and community ties from linking people-in-places to linking people at any place. Computer-supported communication is every*where*, but it is situated no*where*. It is I-alone that is reachable wherever I am: at a home, hotel, office, highway, or shopping center. The person has become the portal.[11]

I am now primarily an individual, not part of a traditional grouping. And yet I still need to have an identity, even if it is not as part of a community or grouping based on the old paradigm of geography. And here the Internet has wired us together in surprising new ways and has allowed us all to identify by our personal interests, whatever they happen to be. Shared *interests* rather than shared *space* now define community.

Do you see the shift here? Our perception of community is becoming disembodied, a product of mediated communication based on shared interest rather than a product of face-to-face communication based on shared space.

▪ Networked Individualism

But does all of this communication necessarily mean that we are actually together? In 2003, Barry Wellman coined a useful term that describes who we are in our online communities. He spoke of *networked individualism*, noting that today's users of digital technologies now identify less with local groups and increasingly as parts of geographically scattered networks. Because our technologies tear up the anchors that once bound us to a certain geographical location (a physical street address, a phone number tied to a particular location), we are now free to network in entirely new ways. This gives us a whole new basis for community. Wellman observes, "Rather than relying on a single community for social support, individuals often actively seek out a variety of appropriate people and resources for different situations."[12] Each person can build his own community, not bound by people within a particular geographical area, but bound only by the ability to find them online. Community has become personalized, individualized. We are now networked together, not as a network of small traditionally defined groups, but as a network of individuals.

This term, *networked individualism*, has another sense, though, another facet of meaning. Because our communities are based on shared interests rather than shared space, we are networked as a group of individuals who have fluid identities. Because our connections are ethereal and virtual rather than bound by geography, we can leave a community without any fear of consequences, without being concerned about a knock on the door from a concerned friend or pastor. As individuals we form our communities, and as individuals we leave them. And so we are networked as individuals who are more concerned with our own interests than those of others — the people in the communities we inhabit. Without the traditional ties of geography or genetics, we have less reason to care for our communities, to nurture them, to be concerned with their long-term strength and success.

I was once part of a very close-knit online community, one bound together by shared interest in a certain hobby. For years I shared much of my life with people through an online forum, sharing joy and pain. I was vocal as a Christian and appreciated for my convictions. For years we nurtured friendships. And then one day, with almost no warning, the website just shut down, disappeared. And what was remarkable to me was how little I cared. The relationships that I had thought were so deep were shown to be very shallow. With the ethereal tie of the website gone — the thing that had tied us together — we all just went our own ways with very little sense of loss. It turned out that we were not much of a community at all, but simply a group of individuals networked together for a time.

While it may be that we have always identified in some sense with communities that were outside of the contexts of home, work, school or church, what has changed today is that for many of us, our *primary* context, our primary identity, is now found elsewhere, in a context unhinged from geography, from the who's or what's closest to us. Many of us are more concerned with who we are in a mediated context than who we are before those who live in the same neighborhood or who attend the same church. Our mediated communities, the ones that exist only in the form of communication—these are the ones we love the most and the ones for which we feel the most.

What happens when this begins to be the case with church?

▪ Real Church and Cyberchurch

A church family is unique among the communities we find in the world. While other communities may be bound together by common interest or common space, churches are bound together by shared belief and, even more so, the common presence of the Holy Spirit. As men and women respond to God's call and turn to him, the Holy Spirit indwells them, binding them together as a family. While genetic families come and go, grow up and peter out, this family will span eternity. While every Christian family wishes to have children, all Christian parents plead that their children would become spiritual brothers and sisters.

Church is changing in this digital age. The titles of books like *The Church of Facebook* and *SimChurch* hint at the kinds of issues we are dealing with as Christians. *SimChurch* asks how we can be the church, how we can be Christ's body, even in a virtual world. Douglas Estes provides a utopian vision for virtual churches, stating, "This type of church is unlike any church the world has ever seen. It has the power to break down social barriers, unite believers from all over the world, and build the kingdom of God with a widow's mite of financing. It is a completely different type of church from any the world has ever seen."[13] He describes the movement of the church from the real world into the virtual world as an evolutionary process. Contrasting virtual churches with the radio and TV ministries of old, he writes, "Virtual churches are products of two inexhaustible torrents redirecting twenty-first-century human development: the exponential rate of technological growth, and postmodernism. The confluence of these two great streams is creating a fertile floodplain for virtual churches to grow in. These churches will not be shadows of real-world churches, recorded and podcast, but something entirely new."[14] Though he does not believe that real-world churches will disappear, he does foresee that many segments of society will migrate to online churches, and some will *only* belong to online church communities.

I fear that he is right.

I fear this because despite arguments to the contrary, the virtual church is *not* the real church.

▪ Christian Love

The book of Acts describes the earliest days of the church as being beautiful in fellowship and in simplicity. It was a community of Christians who "devoted themselves to the apostles' teaching and fellowship, to the breaking of bread and the prayers." The believers were close to one another and were exceedingly generous, "selling their possessions and belongings and distributing the proceeds to all, as any had need. And day by day, attending the temple together and breaking bread in their homes, they received their food with glad and generous hearts, praising God and having favor with all the people." These words are not merely descriptive, but also prescriptive, giving us a picture of how God wants his church to function. It is *because* of this fellowship and community, not apart from it, that we read "And the Lord added to their number day by day those who were being saved" (Acts 2:42–47). God richly blessed them, glorifying himself through their faithfulness and love.

What is clear from Acts is that the church was a community of people who lived in close fellowship with one another. They were a community built on a shared love for God and for one another. This mutual love was expressed as they opened their homes to others and shared what they had.

In the book of Hebrews, we read of another church, one that was struggling in its love. "And let us consider how to stir up one another to love and good works, not neglecting to meet together, as is the habit of some, but encouraging one another, and all the more as you see the Day drawing near" (Hebrews 10:24–25). Here the author of the letter, a pastor to the church, tells the people not to cease meeting together as a fellowship of believers. It appears that the pastor had observed a weakening of the fellowship and interpreted the loss of physical presence as a sign of diminishing love for one another. A lack of concern for the well-being of other Christians is a symptom of self-love. "Selfishness and divisiveness go hand in hand; for self-love breeds the spirit of isolationism. He who does not love his fellow Christians fervently from the heart (1 Peter 1:22) feels no compelling need to associate himself with them."[15] In this church, the failure of love was displayed in a visible way: the people were neglecting to meet together. "It is important, therefore, that the reality of Christian love should be demonstrated in the personal relationships and mutual concerns of the Christian community."[16] Love promotes fellowship, says the author of this letter, but it is equally true that fellowship promotes love. They cannot be neatly separated.

The author of Hebrews tells us that if we are to stir up one another so that we become marked by mutual love and good deeds, we must continue to experience true fellowship face-to-face. The author knows nothing of mediated community, and he would tell us that even if it has benefits, it is never a substitute for the real thing. In fact, the very act of writing his letter proves his point. He tells the church that he would much rather be with them (face-to-face), but he cannot; therefore, a letter will have to suffice (13:18–19, 23). In his unfortunate but necessary absence, he is sending them his written words. We often see this in the writings of Paul as well, as when he writes to the church in Thessalonica, "But since we were torn away from you, brothers, for a short time, in person not in heart, we endeavored the more eagerly and with great desire to see you face to face" (1 Thessalonians 2:17). Mediated presence is good, but face-to-face communication is better. If we are to be a community of Christian love, we must not neglect meeting together.

▪ Christian Community

Bill is twenty years older than I am, though because I got married young and he got married a bit older, our children are around the same ages. Apart from the fact that we each have young children, there is very little else that Bill and I have in common. He is an engineer and I am a writer; he homeschools his children, while mine are enrolled in public schools; he cares nothing for professional sports, while I enjoy them a lot. Bill and I couldn't be more different, and yet I count him as a good friend. I am also friends with Thushara, a bus driver who grew up in Sri Lanka and only recently moved to Canada, and I am friends with Caroline, a dancer who is so much younger and cooler and culturally savvy than I am.

I am joined in community and close fellowship with each of these people. It is Christ who gives us common ground. Without our shared faith, there is little likelihood that our lives would ever overlap or that we would have ever developed a genuine and deep friendship through which we love one another, pray for one another, break bread with one another. But through Christ and because of Christ, we are brothers and sisters; we are friends. And I am so grateful for Christ's grace. We did not deliberately choose to be in community with one another or to be friends. God, in his wisdom, brought us into the same community of believers and has now given us friendship on that basis. This diversity gives just a glimpse at what God is doing in the world. He is building a community of people from every nation, tribe, and tongue and bringing them together in a family that spans the globe and the ages. Each local church is to be a localized manifestation of what he is doing. The diversity of this mysterious body is a reflection of God's own love of diversity and his commitment to save men and women from among every people group in the world.

In theory and in our hearts we know that Christ is doing all of this. But in practice many of us prefer to be individuals and prefer to surround ourselves by others who are as much like us as possible. The more society emphasizes our uniqueness, our individuality, the more difficult we find it to embrace diversity. The same individualistic mind-set that causes us to custom-build our communities of interest, the same technology that allows us to do so, encourages us to custom-build our churches. This includes the online, virtual church.

In *A Journey Worth Taking*, Charles Drew provides an important warning about the involuntary nature of the community God calls us to as his people. He cautions us against elevating our individual tastes in the churches we attend.

> "Church" is not an event. It is people—people whom God calls us to love. What is more, it is in a very important sense an involuntary community of people: we don't choose our brothers and sisters—God does. And sometimes (oftentimes) those people are not terribly compatible with us—not the people we would choose to hang out with. But it is this very incompatibility that is so important, for at least two reasons. First, learning to love the people I don't like is by far the best way to learn how to love (it's easy to love people I happen to like). Second, the church is supposed to be a sociological miracle—a demonstration that Jesus has died and risen to create a new humanity composed of all sorts of people.[17]

God is building a community that is involuntary—one for which *he* determines the membership. Here we get to display to the whole world this sociological miracle that God is working. And it is in the context of this community of people who may be vastly different from us that we are to learn to love one another even more than we love ourselves. We are to worship with one another and love one another on the basis of our common humanity and on the basis of our shared kinship in the family of God rather than on the basis of preference or perceived compatibility. It can be difficult to love those who are unlike us, which is exactly why God calls us to do so. And we are to love them as the Bible instructs us to—through real-life situations, in the real world, from house to house, even in the laying down of our lives for one another. No mediated virtual church can do this. None can replace it, improve on it, or even provide the barest shadow of it. The mediated community will span the limitation of space, but it must do so at the cost of immediacy, of true presence, of the truest manifestations of love.

Are there any benefits, then, from involvement in an online, virtual church community? Let's be practical here. It may be that there are some people who, for one reason or another, are unable to attend church or cannot find a church where the gospel is preached. In such cases, an online church may be a way for them to hear good preaching and to communicate with other Christians. I do not deny that there is some benefit for them. But here we find that the exception proves the rule. Such people will necessarily long for true church and true community, knowing that the online church is but a concession to unavoidable circumstances. It is *never* a replacement for the real thing.

A Lesson from a Brother

In the months that I worked on this book, I listened to the audio version of Brother Andrew's old book *God's Smuggler*. Though Brother Andrew is known primarily for his work in smuggling Bibles into Communist countries during the days of the Cold War, there was another critical component to his work behind the Iron Curtain. As he went from nation to nation, he visited churches and pastors, bringing them greetings from the Christians on the other side of the Curtain, Christians from the free world. This was a ministry of encouragement that became almost as important as his work of delivering Bibles. The greetings he brought to the churches assured the tiny pockets of Christians that they had not been forgotten. Men and women would weep to learn that their brothers and sisters in Christ, though a world away, were praying for them. It was his presence among them that assured them of this, that spoke of the depth of this Christian love.

Though Brother Andrew was God's smuggler, he was also God's envoy, his representative. As he stood there in flesh and blood, standing in nations that denied the existence of God and sought to destroy Christ's body on earth, he stood as a physical manifestation that the church would survive and that the family was intact. This was not something he could do through a letter on paper or a message on a screen. It was *his presence* that mattered more than his words. There he was, *im-mediately* before them, a display of love and Christian fellowship.

In an electronic, mediated world, let's not neglect the privilege and responsibility we have to be real people in a real world. E-mail and text messaging are inevitable aspects of life, and there is no reason to forsake them altogether. But let's keep them in their proper context as *supplemental* and lesser forms of communication. We may well find that if we are to fulfill God's mandate on earth, we will need to communicate less often so we can communicate more. We will need to forsake the ease and the pace of quantity for the reflective significance of quality.

APPLICATION
Mediated Relationships

"Let's not neglect the responsibility we have to be real people in a real world."

To do this, let's look again to our three circles and find just one of the ways we can relate them to the issue of mediation.

We *experience* increasing amounts of mediation in this digital world. We experience so much of it that for many of us it is now the dominant form of communication; we are more mediated than face-to-face. And more and more people are finding that there is a real comfort and familiarity in this. Many of us rely on mediated communication, not just out of necessity, but also out of preference.

In the realm of *theory*, we know that there is a biological component to technology, that a sea change taking us from face-to-face interaction to mediated interaction may affect us in very profound ways. And we know that the medium is the message, that the ways in which we communicate have just as much impact as the content of those communications.

And when we turn to the Bible, to *theology*, we see that some of the great promises of Scripture point us to the joy and the privilege of face-to-face interaction—that communicating in mediated ways is a concession rather than an ideal. It tells us that God is calling us to be communities of real people in the real world—communities that display the diversity of this great family God is building out of all tongues and all nations.

So let's talk about mediation and what it is about *more* mediation, rather than *less* mediation, that draws so many of us. What is it about mediation that gives it such strong appeal? Why is it that in a digital world we migrate from real-world communities to online communities, that we hear of more and more people heading to online churches, that so many of us prefer to send an e-mail or text message than make a phone call or knock on a door?

We've lost the big picture. Even Christians have become pragmatic when it comes to communication. We allow what is convenient to overrule what may be better or best. We have not thought carefully and deliberately about issues related to mediation (which is exactly why I've sought to do so in this book). Without the big picture to guide us and give us understanding, we have fallen into unhealthy patterns. Our ignorance has led us astray.

Mediated communication is easy and safe. As our communication with one another becomes increasingly mediated, communication that involves more of us feels too intimate, too intimidating, too difficult. Journalist Ian Shapira writes, "Young people say they avoid voice calls because the immediacy of a phone call strips them of the control that they have over the arguably less-intimate pleasures of texting, e-mailing, Facebooking, or tweeting. They even complain that phone calls are by their nature impolite, more of an interruption than the blip of an arriving text."[18] Isn't it interesting that phone calls represent an interruption, and an intimate kind of interruption at that? As more-mediated communication becomes the norm (think text messaging), less-mediated contact (the telephone) becomes more intimate and, therefore, more difficult. We prefer what requires less of us ahead of what requires more.

Mediated communication requires less focus and time. Digital communication allows us to focus on more than one thing at a time. Deborah Tannen, a linguistics professor at Georgetown University who studies how people converse in everyday life, tells of a student who "told me that it takes her days to call her parents back and the parents thought she was intentionally putting them off. But the parents didn't get it. It's the medium. With e-mails, you're at the computer, writing a paper. With phone calls, it's a dedicated block of time."[19] In a world with so much distraction, a world of near-constant communication, it is difficult to dedicate time to one person at a time and one task at a time. Mediated communication gives us the ability to dedicate less of ourselves to more people.

Mediated communication gives us greater control. Ultimately, many of the issues related to mediation come down to control. Much of what appeals to us in digital life is the illusion of control it gives us. Life online tends to be much less messy, much more predictable, than life in the world of flesh and blood. Digital technology offers us a life we can take or leave on our own terms and according to our own criteria. It lets us personalize our lives and our relationships, to respond to what we want when we want to. By looking at pornography, we can control our sexual encounters, never having to deal with a spouse who has a headache and never having a partner say, "No, I don't want to do that." By worshiping at a cyberchurch, we can control who worships alongside of us; we can control our commitment, showing up only when we want and participating only as much as we desire; we can control our time, choosing the time and date that works best for us.

By giving us control, our new technologies tend to enhance existing idols in our lives. Instead of becoming more like Christ through the forming and shaping influence of a church community, we form and shape and personalize our community to make it more like us. We take control of things that are not ours to control.

But God never calls us to a life of ease, a life in which we maintain control and do things on our own terms. He puts us in marriage relationships, in friendships, in church communities, for his own reasons; he puts us in such relationships to teach us how to love one another and more and more resemble him in his great love. Could it be that our desire for control is short-circuiting the process of change and transformation God wants us to experience through the mess of real-world, flesh-and-blood, face-to-face relationships?

So how, then, do we live in the sweet spot as we communicate? We need to see the superiority of face-to-face communication and prioritize it above what is mediated. We cannot afford to become lazy, to allow pragmatism and convenience and ignorance to define the ways we communicate with one another.

QUESTIONS FOR REFLECTION

1. In what situations do you find that you are prone to rely on mediated communication rather than immediate?

2. Do you agree that the best relationships we can have are those that are predominantly face-to-face? What are some relationships in which you have been migrating away from the face-to-face? Why?

3. In what ways do you find that you prefer your online self to your offline self? What is it about your online self that appeals to you?

4. What are some examples of your own migration away from community defined by space in order to dedicate yourself to an online community based on shared interests? What have been some of the positive aspects of this experience? What have been some of the negative aspects?

CHAPTER 6

TURN OFF
and
TUNE IN
(Distraction)

Beeeeeeep.

You know the sound well. It begins and ends with the twin plosives *b* and *p* and in between offers an *eee* that lasts as long as we care to make it. It may well be that when we read a history of our times, the beep will be the defining noise of a generation. The beep is a purely human sound, one without any equivalent in nature.[1] No animal, no plant, makes a beep.

That beep can be a dot or a dash, a mere blip or a long and sustained sound. It can make itself known just once, or it can repeat endlessly. We hear the beep in many different contexts: our phones beep, e-mail beeps, trucks beep as they back up, washers beep when a load of clothes is clean. No matter the context, the message is always the same: "Pay attention to me!" Beeps always demand a response, even if the response is only to silence an irritating noise. We may need to look up from what we are doing and press a button; we may need to sprint out of the way of a moving truck; we may need to throw some clothes into the dryer—but in every case, a beep calls us to action. It calls us *from* one thing and *to* another.

The beep is undiscerning and thoughtless. It calls us out of sleep and reverie, out of church and school; it demands our attention as we stand vigil at the deathbed of a loved one. Every beep exacts a cost, whether the cost is simply the brief moment of distraction as our attention turns to the source of the noise, or the necessity of running from imminent danger. These beeps fill our lives. Often, they run our lives.

This book was far more difficult for me to write than the last one I wrote just three years earlier. My dependence on technology has increased, and there are new and creative ways for me to be distracted. The beeps in my life have grown and increased in number. Often, in the midst of writing, I was distracted by the beeps and buzzes and flashing lights telling me that something is waiting for my attention, something is calling for me, drawing me to notice it. Beeps tell me that I am needed elsewhere. And far too often, I obey and answer the call. Eventually, I had to find new and creative ways of getting out of the flow, of flipping switches off and taking control again. I had to silence the torrent of beeps in my life so I could focus, at least for a time, and work undistracted from interruptions. Only then could I truly think.

Just before writing this chapter, in the summer of 2010, I went away on a week's vacation. This was the first time I had chosen to escape not just my home but also my media—to escape both my geographical *and* digital worlds. I drove with my family some 650 miles south to a state park in the middle of Virginia and stayed there for a week with no e-mail, no cell phone signal, no Facebook or Twitter or television or computer games.

And there were no beeps.

Immediately, I noticed that the loss of my digital technologies had slowed the pace of my life. No longer were these devices beckoning to me, demanding that I respond to them, calling me to answer e-mails and respond to messages. For a full week, I left behind the harried world of modern digital life. It actually took me several days to respond to this new pace of life and grow comfortable moving at this slower pace. Unfortunately, upon my return it took only a few hours to turn things on once again and increase the speed.

While staying at the cabin in the woods of Virginia, I was able to clearly see the level of distraction in my life, the distraction of digital living. It is increasingly difficult to remain undistracted when every new technology seems to evolve toward greater distraction. In an essay on the related topics of distraction and procrastination, Paul Graham writes, "Distraction is not a static obstacle that you avoid like you might avoid a rock in the road. Distraction seeks you out."[2] Like the beeps that emanate from our digital devices, the technology of our time is bent on seeking us out, finding us wherever we are, and drawing us somewhere else.

On the one hand, we have become somewhat dependent on our devices. After all, they bring us great benefits. We are not ready to give them up. But on the other hand, we must honestly face the truth that these devices are prone to draw us away from the important things in life — and the people who are closest to us. The cell phone, a device meant to enhance my communication with others, can increase my ability to communicate with those who are *far* from me, often at the cost of communication with my own wife and children — those *closest* to me.

Eventually the problem of distraction becomes more than something that just happens to us; it defines our identity. We become distracted people. We begin to flit from one thing to the next, whether or not there is a beep to summon us. We become so shaped by our devices that we lose our ability to focus. We are transformed from people who *respond* to the beep to people *of* the beep.

The Danger of Distraction

If we are a distracted people, a distracted society, it stands to reason that we would also be a distracted church, a church with a diminished ability to think deeply, to cultivate concentration, to emphasize slow, deliberate, thoughtful meditation. What Paul said of the unbelieving Jews of his day could likely be said of many of us today: "I bear them witness that they have a zeal for God, but not according to knowledge" (Romans 10:2). Christians may be excited about God, but because they have become a product of our digital world, they have a diminished ability to think deeply about him, to truly know him as he is. More and more of us are finding that we just can't stop long enough to read. We can't sustain our attention long enough to study. We can't find the time to meet with our Father. Where prayer used to be the first activity of the day, we now begin our daily routine by checking e-mail. Where the Bible used to be a special book we read and studied, now it's an e-book that competes with our voice mail, text messages, e-mails, and the ever-present lure of the Internet.

When I speak on the topic of technology to Christian audiences, this is the issue, more than any other, that they have questions about. "Why am I so distracted? Why is life suddenly moving so quickly? Why can't I think anymore?" They have begun to experience the fruit of constant distraction, but they don't have a theoretical or theological structure in place to make sense of how it is happening or how to respond. Their minds are scattered, and they're desperate for help.

Here is one of the great dangers we face as Christians: With the ever-present distractions in our lives, we are quickly becoming a people of shallow thoughts, and shallow thoughts will lead to shallow living. There is a simple and inevitable progression at work here:

Distraction —> Shallow Thinking —> Shallow Living

All of this distraction is reshaping us in two dangerous ways. First, we are tempted to forsake quality for quantity, believing the lie that virtue comes through speed, productivity, and efficiency. We think that more must be better, and so we drive ourselves to do more, accomplish more, *be* more. And second, as this happens, we lose our ability to engage in deeper ways of thinking—concentrated, focused thought that requires time and cannot be rushed. Instead of focusing our efforts in a *few* directions, we give scant attention to many things, skimming instead of studying. We live rushed lives and forget how to move slowly, carefully, and thoughtfully through life.

The challenge facing us is clear. We need to relearn how to think, and we need to discipline ourselves to think deeply, conquering the distractions in our lives so that we can *live* deeply. We must rediscover how to be truly thoughtful Christians, as we seek to live with virtue in the aftermath of the digital explosion.

Identifying Our Distraction

We must first learn to identify the nature of our distraction and understand how distraction has become more than just an isolated bother but a pervasive presence. Before we do this, however, we must understand two crucial factors—two cultural understandings and emphases that have shifted in response to the rise of digital technology: our changed understanding of time and space, and the modern virtues of speed and capacity.

▪ Time and Space

As mankind has sought to carry out God's mandate and exercise dominion over the world, he has had to gain control over the elements of time and space. Time has been tamed by measurement. Consider that Adam and Eve weren't created with the sense of time that we take for granted today (particularly in the Western world). They didn't think in terms of hours and minutes. They knew sunup and sundown, the cool of the evening hour and the heat of the midday sun. As man advanced and began carrying out the creation mandate, he learned to divide time into useful segments — years, months, weeks, days, and hours. By measuring time, we have been able to bring a sense of order to our lives and societies.

Man has also faced the limitations imposed by space, by our distance from one another, and these have been tamed through our growing ability to communicate over vast distances. Through writing, and then later by means of the printing press and the radio, our understanding of space has changed as we have learned to communicate far beyond the reach of the human voice. A postcard can extend my voice from my home office in Oakville, Canada, to my friend's kitchen in Kurri Kurri, Australia.

And what a blessing it is that God has allowed us to have dominion over time and space! Because we understand the concept of time and are able to measure it, we now have the ability to agree on a 10:00 a.m. church service so we can meet together in worship and Christian fellowship. Because we have conquered space, we are able to read the Bible, whether it is printed on paper or displayed in pixels on a screen.

Our control over time and space has brought greater control over our lives. We are able to be where we want when we want to be there, and we are able to communicate at almost any time or place. Yet the growth of our understanding of time and space has always come at a cost (but by now you know that, right?). Such shifts inevitably change the way we understand ourselves and are often accompanied by some form of social upheaval.

This was true when the mechanical clock first appeared in monasteries in the Middle Ages. The chimes from such clocks were heard in nearby towns, and the people in those communities soon found themselves structuring their days around them. Centuries later, in the era of industrialization, factories introduced the concept of a highly structured workday. Communications professor Jarice Hanson writes, "During the industrial revolution, factory owners adopted the clock as the regulator of all human activity on the assembly line, and the concept that 'time was money' dictated social relations in the factory."[3] This in turn generated widespread social change—factory workers were now expected to show up for work at a set hour and to work until a specific time, with deviations punished by fines or dismissal. Today we take such things for granted; in its time it was revolutionary. It changed human society; it changed how we saw ourselves.

As technology has evolved, so too has our understanding of time, and with it our belief that we have control over time. Digital time is inherent in all of our digital devices, most of which run on processors defined by their clock speed, and such devices have allowed us to divide time into tiny little fragments, down from seconds into milliseconds and units far smaller than that. Olympic events used to be measured in seconds and half seconds; today many events are measured in thousandths of seconds, forty times faster than the blink of an eye.

One of the ways in which digital clocks have changed the way we understand time is by removing any sense of the past and future in favor of the precision of the moment. Ask a person who wears an old-fashioned analog watch the time, and he might say, "Quarter to three." Ask the same question of a person with a digital watch, and he might say, "Two forty-four and twenty-three seconds." Inherent in the analog clock, a *synchronous* measure of time, is a sense of the past and the future. One glance shows time past and time to come as the hands sweep across the face of the clock.

In his study of the effects of our understanding of time, anthropologist Edward T. Hall shows that an analog, a synchronous understanding of time, fosters the belief that we can only do one thing at a time.[4] Its sense of past and future, of time that is gone and time that will soon be here, leads us to have a realistic sense of what we can accomplish right now. But inherent in the digital clock, an *asynchronous* measure, is a nonlinear sense of time, stripping the present moment from any kind of continuity with the past or future. There is only *right now*. Our digital technologies and understanding of time give us little scope of past or future. Jarice Hanson observes, "Digital time encourages us to think in fragments, with little connection to a sense of process."[5] In this way, digital technology contributes to our feeling that we can and must accomplish *many things at once*; we are inclined to see only the present and all of its immediate demands. And in the present moment we find ourselves overwhelmed with responsibilities, overwhelmed with things to do, yet still trying to do more.

While our understanding of time has been affected by the digital explosion, so too has our sense of place. The Greek philosopher Plato once expressed great concern that the technology of writing would change our understanding of space. He believed that writing things down would destroy our memories and that the simple act of recalling written facts would become more important than truly understanding such facts and applying them to life.

Perhaps he was right.

If anything, the digital explosion has only further changed our understanding of space. Perhaps you can still remember those days when each family had a single telephone that would serve the entire household. It was usually located in a central location such as the kitchen, and a person who called that particular phone would say, "Hello, is John there?" When we called, we were asking if John was *there*, if he was present in a certain place, because we knew we could only communicate with him if that were the case. If John was down the street or at the ballgame, we could not talk to him; we would have to wait until he returned. Today, though, we call John on his cell phone and talk to him, whether he is at home, at the ballgame, or halfway across the world. Similarly, we used to send letters to a person at a particular fixed and physical address, while today we send e-mails that the person can receive, whether he is in America or Afghanistan. We have disconnected our ability to communicate from any conception of space. And as communication technologies allowed us to conquer space, change inevitably followed.

Not surprisingly, the digital explosion has radically altered our sense of time and space, changing and shaping us along the way. Many of us no longer have a personal home phone and a work cell phone — we have a single device that does it all. When this is the case, we cannot be surprised when we receive work calls at home and personal calls at work, when we act like workers in the home and like homemakers at work.

Our devices keep us in touch all day, every day. The distracted state they bring is not always incidental or accidental. In many cases it is deliberately imposed on us as an intended consequence. The purpose of a multifunction device like the iPhone, providing a world of functions and applications, is to stop its owner whenever and wherever he is in order to pull him from one thing to the next. As soon as he takes a call, it provides him with a reminder from his calendar; and when he responds to that reminder, he receives an e-mail; and when he replies to the e-mail, he receives a text message. And so it goes, from one distraction to the next. This is exactly what the iPhone is meant to do. And it does it well.

A recent study by Synovate found that more than 4 in 10 Americans say they can't live without their mobile phone; 82 percent say they never leave home without it; nearly half of them sleep with it nearby.[6] It is not enough for them to send text messages all day; they need to have their phones with them in case something happens during the night. Meanwhile, more and more of us are taking our cell phones and computers on vacation with us, mixing work time with leisure time. Just glance around your church on a Sunday morning, and you may well notice people sending text messages during worship. During a time of singing at a recent conference, I spotted a woman raising one hand in worship while sending a text message with the other one. We mix worship with our work and pleasure. Why are we surprised when we can only give partial attention to any one of them?

We sought to conquer time and space to exercise dominion, to control the creation for our own benefit. Somewhere along the way the tables have been turned. We are now the ones being controlled. It's no wonder, then, that we are so distracted. We are slaves to our own inventions.

▪ Speed and Capacity

For centuries, humans have been captivated by the possibility of a perpetual motion machine, an invention that could provide a never-ending source of motion or energy while requiring no external source of power. The principles of the laws of thermodynamics have since shown us that, as far as we understand the laws of nature, such machines are impossible. Yet inventors continue to try to create them; the allure and the potential reward are simply too great to ignore. But while perpetual motion *machines* may be only the stuff of fantasy, our technologies seem to be successful in making us perpetual motion *people*. While the Industrial Revolution turned man into a machine, digitization has imposed on him the identity of constant activity, of never-ending motion.

When we buy a new digital device, it is typically described in reference to speed and capacity. When I go shopping for a new laptop, I find that the processor operates at a certain clock speed, that faster is always better, and that this in turn will give me a greater capacity to perform complex operations. Never mind that most of us will never tap into all of that speed or even need more than a fraction of the capacity—more is simply better. With our increased speeds and capacities we know we are getting a better deal, earning more bang for our buck.

But what if this emphasis on speed and capacity has begun to shape us?

What if our consumption and use of these devices has trained us to assume that greater speed and greater capacity are universal virtues? What if we have transferred the virtues of digital devices to our own lives?

The new generation of any device will inevitably be faster than the ones that came before, and the promise is that this will empower us to accomplish *more* things in *less* time. The discerning consumer may wonder why, if computers are twice as fast as they used to be, he doesn't get his work finished in half the time! But it is difficult to stop to ask such questions. The pressure of life is such that if we don't embrace the newer and better, we will be left behind. Because of this, our devices are obsolete long before they stop working. Instead of asking thoughtful questions—exercising discernment over our use of digital technology—we press on, trying to match the speed of our new devices, absorbing into our consciousness the idea that speed itself is a virtue, that fast is always good. We recreate ourselves in the image of our devices, through the ideologies they contain within them.

The speed of digital life, the understanding that e-mails grow stale if they are not responded to immediately, the knowledge that a text message that is a few hours old is already ancient, increases the pace of our lives. Eventually we begin trying to make everything faster. We try to speed up our families, our worship, our eating. We begin to race through life, unwilling or perhaps unable to slow down, to pause, and to reflect.

And yet when we turn to the Bible, when we turn to the source of divine wisdom, we see very little about a life dominated by more, dominated by speed. On the contrary, we look to our heroes—we look to our Savior—and see a life that is contemplative, a life that takes time to ponder the deep things.

King Solomon was the wisest man who ever lived, and his life gave little indication of speed. Rather, his life showed the virtue of deliberate meditation, deliberate slowness. He knew 3,000 proverbs, each of which took time to commit to memory and each of which only had value in the time taken to ponder it. Here is just one example of how Solomon grew in wisdom and understanding:

> I passed by the field of a sluggard,
>   by the vineyard of a man lacking sense,
> and behold, it was all overgrown with thorns;
>   the ground was covered with nettles,
>   and its stone wall was broken down.
> Then I saw and considered it;

I looked and received instruction.
A little sleep, a little slumber,
  a little folding of the hands to rest,
and poverty will come upon you like a robber,
  and want like an armed man.

Proverbs 24:30–34

Here Solomon walks by a field and pauses to observe that it has become overgrown with thorns and that the wall surrounding it has fallen into decay. He sees that only a lazy man, a sluggard, a fool, would allow his land to fall into such a state. Even in the midst of his busy life as king, Solomon responds by taking the time to meditate on this, to consider it. And having done so, he receives divine instruction: "A little sleep, a little slumber, a little folding of the hands to rest, and poverty will come upon you like a robber, and want like an armed man." It was only through his willingness to slow down, to take time, that he drew a lesson from this foolish man and his misused land. Virtue was found not in hastening by but in taking time to slow down, to pause, to think. He did not immediately dash off a Twitter update or snap a photo to post to Facebook. He stopped; he watched; he learned.

Speed is just one of the ways we measure ourselves. We also measure ourselves by our capacity, by our ability to produce. Just as our devices continually evolve toward greater capacity, so too we demand more and more of ourselves. We want to keep up with our devices; we want to be productive, to use each moment of each day to accomplish something tangible. The emphasis on productivity arose during the period of industrialization, when factory owners realized that they could generate a more profitable product if they ruthlessly controlled every aspect of its production. And so they hired experts who watched and measured every aspect of production until every moment of every worker's day was regulated and accounted for. Every person was required to be productive in every moment. What did not directly and obviously contribute to profit had to be culled. As a society, and especially as a digital society that places great emphasis on capacity, we have absorbed and enhanced this mind-set in which we constantly demand productivity of ourselves and of our devices. We associate our own productivity with our devices, sure that they will make us more capable of doing more and better work. And so we take our computers with us on vacations so we can keep up with our customers; we expect that our coworkers will check work e-mails away from the desk; we have BlackBerrys that tie us to the office at any time and in any place.

Christians have long understood that productivity is not easily measured by any spiritual metric. And when we turn to the Bible we see little demand for constant productivity. We read of Jesus, who maintained a ministry in which he was always in demand. As he went from one town to the next, the crowds pressed around him, asking him to go this way and that, to heal the sick, to cure the lame. And yet Jesus constantly retreated. He would go into the wilderness by himself for extended periods of quiet communion with his Father; he would enjoy an intimate dinner with a handful of friends; he would gather his few disciples around him and savor their company. As the pace grew, Jesus would constantly slow it down in order to keep his focus on what was most important. Where we might keep count of the number of people Jesus healed and those who professed him as Lord—and measure Jesus' productivity in this way—he kept himself accountable to a higher measure. Much of his time was not productive in any way we could easily measure. And yet his time was sacred, every moment dedicated to the Father.

Few of us today have such self-control, such dedication to what matters most. Re-created in the image of speedy and productive devices, we find meaning in speed and constant productivity. Yet many of us wish that life would slow down and become less overwhelming. We know that there must be something more than the constant distraction, the constant velocity.

Shallow Thinking

Our desire for speed and productivity has made it nearly impossible to dedicate time to thought and meditation. Instead, we find that we succumb to shallow thinking. Such shallow thinking becomes increasingly hard to combat when we become people who multitask and seek to learn, not by reading, but by skimming.

▪ Multitasking

The demand for speed and capacity pushes us to want to do *more* things and to do more *faster*. When we combine these two factors we uncover one of the great virtues of modern life, something we are all familiar with: *efficiency*. We do not just want to do things quickly and constantly; we want to do *even more things* quickly and constantly. We want to be efficient so we can accomplish even more, faster. Books on efficiency regularly make their way to the bestseller lists, and they promise to aid us as we try to squeeze the most we can get out of every moment—to get as much done as possible in as little time as possible so we can do more things just as quickly. Along the way, though, we necessarily sacrifice quality in favor of quantity, depth in favor of width.

One way we pursue the virtue of efficiency is by becoming multitaskers. If we are driven by efficiency, it is not enough that we work quickly; we must also work on many things simultaneously. Imitating our computers, we seek to switch seamlessly from one task to the next, from one priority to another. At our desks we work on our projects while chatting on instant messengers, sending off text messages, and glancing at our favorite blogs. Even in our entertainment we want to be able to do many things at once—to be able to watch television while sending a text message and checking in on our friends' Facebook pages.

A rash of recent studies shows that multitasking is not a solution. In fact, studies show that multitasking is actually a misnomer. While we think we are multitasking, we are actually task switching, doing a little bit of one thing and then doing a little bit of another. Our brains just won't allow us to perform two complex operations at the same time with the same skill. Quality necessarily suffers, as does depth. Not only that, but multitasking is not even very efficient. David E. Meyer, a psychology professor at the University of Michigan, found that "people who switch back and forth between two tasks, like exchanging e-mail and writing a report, may spend 50 percent more time on those tasks than if they work on them separately, completing one before starting the other."[7]

Meanwhile, if we surround ourselves by too many stimuli, we force our brains into a state of continuous partial attention, a state in which we keep tabs on everything without giving focused attention to anything. When in this state of continuous partial attention, "people may place their brains in a heightened state of stress. They no longer have time to reflect, contemplate, or make thoughtful decisions. Instead, they exist in a sense of constant crisis—on alert for a new contact or bit of exciting news or information at any moment. Once people get used to this state, they tend to thrive on the perpetual connectivity. It feeds their egos and sense of self-worth, and it becomes irresistible."[8]

Whether through multitasking or through monitoring so many sources of input that we remain in continuous partial attention, we lose the ability to think in a sustained way. Many teachers today remark that students are unable to sustain a single thought or theme for more than one paragraph.

They will write a paragraph and then pause to check in with their friends or to dash off a few text messages. Then they return to their essay, but already they have lost their context. The next paragraph has no real relation to the one before.[9] Even as I wrote the early drafts of this chapter, before I learned to shut off sources of input, I noticed that the chapter was fragmented and scattered, showing clear evidence of too many interruptions and too little focus.

As our technologies promote speed and capacity, the ability to do more in less time, they may promote a new form of idolatry. They push us to make productivity and efficiency ends in themselves, idols we worship and serve. We elevate efficiency—the need to get many things done, and to get them done quickly—to the realm of the ultimate. We willingly sacrifice quality, relationships, and our devotion to those we love in order to fulfill this twisted mandate.

The Bible emphasizes and values, unsurprisingly, not speed or efficiency, but quality and the motivation of our heart. True virtue is found not by getting a task finished quickly but by getting it done and doing it well. Virtue comes in fulfilling God's mandate to do all things for his glory, not in doing many things at once. As we work to the best of our ability, it is not always necessary to get it done quickly or to produce vast quantities. Our goal is to honor him: "Whether you eat or drink, or whatever you do, do all to the glory of God" (1 Corinthians 10:31). It is not speed, productivity, or efficiency that matter—it is the heart.

This is as true in worship as it is in the workplace. Efficiency is a dangerous mind-set to bring to our faith. We do not want to be *efficient* worshipers, driven by a desire to get more of God in a shorter amount of time. We do not want to be *hurried* worshipers who value speed over quality. And yet there are multitudes of One Minute Bibles and Two Minute Devotionals available for those of us who just can't spare the time, for those who need a spiritual fix for the sake of conscience but aren't willing to sacrifice more time. Despite our best efforts, we cannot escape the truth: quality time *is* quantity time. We need to be Christians who take time to give sustained focus to one thing—the worship of the living God. He does not call us to study his Word or to worship him more efficiently. God calls us to read his Word *meditatively*, to give it the time and attention it needs—the attention *we* need—if the Word is to pierce "to the division of soul and of spirit, of joints and of marrow, and discerning the thoughts and intentions of the heart" (Hebrews 4:12).

▪ Skimming

Sadly, in addition to multitasking, we also find that we have lost the ability to read and study in a sustained way. We have become scanners rather than engagers, skimmers in place of readers.

Studies of Internet users have long shown that websites turn readers into skimmers. When the average user visits a web page, his eyes very quickly scan the page in an F pattern. Beginning at the top left, he scans along the top of the page before jumping down a couple of inches. There he repeats the scan, but this time he may not make it all the way to the right margin. Then he jumps down again toward the bottom of the screen. In this process, which takes just a second or two, he has scanned the page and has made an evaluation of it. Often this is all he will do before hitting the Back button. This is a new ability, and one that has come to us as we've become Internet readers. It is one we've had to develop in order to quickly weigh and evaluate the vast amounts of information available online. This means that most of us "read" and evaluate an entire web page in a matter of just a few seconds, certainly far less time than it would take to actually understand and digest the words.

In this time of transition when we are shifting from the printed word to the pixel word, we still find it difficult to focus on digital content the way we can on printed content. In part, this is because many digital technologies are deliberately training us to skim rather than absorb. The search giant Google has a vested interest in fostering a culture of distraction, encouraging short engagements with a wide variety of information. While we may like to think of Google as a helpful search tool, we cannot forget that it is still a corporation in the business of making money, and Google makes their money by selling advertisements. These ads are everywhere in the Google experience—in the sidebars of the searches, superimposed above videos, in the margins of your e-mails. Carefully filtered to be as relevant as possible to you the user, it is in Google's best interests to have you see as many of these advertisements as possible. After all, the more of them you see, the more likely you are to click on them. And the way they get you to see more ads is by making you see more web pages. They have nothing to gain and dollars to lose if you choose to remain on a single page for an extended period of time.

In an interview with *BusinessWeek*, Irene Au, Google's user experience director, states, "Our goal is to get users in and out really quickly. All our design decisions are based on that strategy."[10] Google's design strategy, always minimal, always with the content density toward the very top of the page, is geared toward having the user move quickly from their site, to the next, and back again. Google wants and needs your experience of the Internet to be as wide and as shallow as possible. They want to feed you snippets of information and to then have you return to their search engine to search some more and to view more ads. Google's profit is not tied to the *quality* of information its users consume, but the *velocity* of it. Author Nicholas Carr observes, "The last thing the company wants is to encourage leisurely reading or slow, concentrated thought. Google is, quite literally, in the business of distraction."[11] They do this even as they attempt to scan all the books in the world and add them to a massive online library. This is not a library of books as much as it is a library of snippets of books, small fragments of text. Having shown that the fragmenting of knowledge, quickly moving people in and out, can be an extraordinarily successful business model, other companies are following in their wake. Few sites have found a way of turning a profit by providing deep and lengthy engagement with their content.

The sites that generate content have long realized that to be successful they need to package their content in short, punchy ways. Users will not read lengthy texts. Instead, they want their information to be distilled to the essence, easily digested in mere seconds. Consuming information is far more important than interacting with it or engaging with it in a meaningful way. Bloggers have long been told that a blog article should be no longer than 250 words since beyond that, most people will skim at best. Many will simply click away and not return.

Admittedly, there is some value in the ability to scan a page. This is a skill many of us learned in school as part of a reading system. It is often quite useful to skim a book before reading it so you can draw out the author's main points and piece together a basic overview of the book before actually reading it. Knowing some of the author's goals and some of what he will teach is an important aid to comprehension and retention. *What is unique in our time, though, is that skimming has now become the dominant form of reading.* No longer a means to an end, it is now the primary way we gather information and make sense of that information.[12] We do not read at a leisurely pace but as quickly as possible, as if gathering information, rather than comprehension and application, is the ultimate goal.

The danger for Christians is apparent. If we grow so accustomed to skimming words, to passing quickly over texts, we will eventually impose this practice on the words of God. The danger today, in an era of skimming and fragmentation, is that we will fragment the Bible into small bits and have no time or ability to craft unity from the parts. "All Scripture is breathed out by God and profitable for teaching, for reproof, for correction, and for training in righteousness" (2 Timothy 3:16). *All* Scripture is profitable; all Scripture is necessary. It is not profitable in isolation, but in its whole, in its unity. And we cannot understand this unity without thought and focus.

Thinking Deeply

In the midst of all of this distraction, the cure is to refocus our attention on what matters most. If our distracted existence is the fruit of allowing beeps to control our lives and of turning speed and capacity into divine virtues, then we must respond by silencing the beeps and relearning how to focus.

▪ The Christian Mind

If ever there has been a religion that has called people to use their minds, it is the Christian faith. If ever there has been a religion that has emphasized the importance of teaching, it is the Christian faith. Many other systems of faith downplay teaching in favor of ritual, stating that doctrine is less important than performance. But the Christian faith requires that Christians use their God-given minds, their God-renewed minds, in order to know what is true and to reject what is false.[13]

Writing to the Colossian church, Paul states:

> And so, from the day we heard, we have not ceased to pray for you, asking that you may be filled with the knowledge of his will in all spiritual wisdom and understanding, so as to walk in a manner worthy of the Lord, fully pleasing to him, bearing fruit in every good work and increasing in the knowledge of God.
>
> Colossians 1:9–10

Note the progression of Paul's prayer. First he prays that these new Christians may be filled with the knowledge of God's will in spiritual wisdom and understanding. He wants them to know about God, to know who God is, to have minds and hearts filled with wisdom and understanding. And why does he want this for them? Because it is only then that they may "walk in a manner worthy of the Lord." If they are to know God, they must first know *about* God. To have obedience, they must first have knowledge. And this knowledge of God and this honoring of God will bear fruit and will, in turn, further their knowledge of God. Paul prays that these people may have Christian minds and that they may *use* their minds.

We are to study God by studying the Word of God, and, on that basis, then to live for him. We are to be like the noble Bereans, who "received the word with all eagerness, examining the Scriptures daily to see if these things were so" (Acts 17:11). These Berean Christians used their minds to search the Bible to ensure that Paul and Silas were teaching the truth.

If we are to do any of this, we will need to work tirelessly to eliminate distractions and to focus on what matters most, without being drawn aside by the beeps and buzzes and the demand for efficiency. God created us in such a way that we naturally respond to stimuli within our environment. When we hear a noise, we listen and respond with a turning of the head; when we see a flashing light, we see and respond with a turning of attention. God created us this way for our own good and protection. Yet too much stimulus can keep us from focusing our attention on one thing. There is good reason that libraries are places of quiet and that there are no strobe lights in church sanctuaries. Christians have long understood the importance of quiet solitude. David knew this, which is why he rose early in the day, before he could be distracted, to spend time alone with God. "My eyes are awake before the watches of the night, that I may meditate on your promise" (Psalm 119:148). David knew that a life of virtue required a life of thoughtful meditation.

David did not have to contend with a cell phone that would ring whether he was awake or asleep, working or worshiping. He did not have to contend with the fast pace of e-mail or text messaging. He did not have to wrestle with whether to begin the day in worship or in checking his Facebook account. If we are to live with virtue in this digital age, we need to recognize that we are engaged in a battle, at war with distraction. We must learn to discover what distracts us, destroy it, cultivate concentration, and seek out solitude regularly and habitually.[14]

Heart, Soul, Mind, Strength

As Christians, we should not be surprised that our technologies often seem to work against us. We know that technology, like everything in creation, is subject to the curse. Distraction will never completely disappear. I have dedicated a lot of time and effort to eliminating distraction from my life, and yet even now I am chatting with a friend on instant messenger as I type these words (it turns out that I forgot to log off before working on this chapter).

As Christians we know that God calls us to live with virtue, to live thoughtfully before him, to use our God-given minds to live in a way that honors him. If we are to take our responsibilities seriously, we must learn to ignore the buzzes, the beeps, and the distractions that threaten to drown out serious thought and reflection. We must learn to remain undistracted, to wholeheartedly focus our attention on the things that matter most, and to love God with all of our heart, soul, *mind*, and strength.

APPLICATION

An Undistracted Life

If we are to live deep lives, lives that truly matter, we must first fill our hearts and minds with deep thoughts, thoughts that truly matter. Distraction is the enemy of deep thinking, and it is an enemy we must seek out and destroy. So let's talk about how we can live in our sweet spot between experience, theory, and theology.

The *experience* of most of us shows that we are increasingly distracted—that we have a million beeps in our lives, each one seeking to draw us from one thing and to another. We are finding that there is a clear correlation between the digital explosion and digital distraction. And our devices are beginning to train us to be distracted people in all areas of life.

The *theory* of technology backs this up. It shows that we create devices in our own image but that they soon seek to return the favor. So we have created devices that will distract us in order to notify us of an incoming call or to remind us of an important appointment. But as our commitment to such devices has grown, they have started to shape us in important ways.

Our *theology* tells us that there is great benefit to remaining undistracted, to focusing our hearts and minds on what matters most. The Bible points us to spiritual heroes who were able to remain undistracted, who were willing to take time to ponder the deep things.

So how can we live in a deep and meaningful way—a way that avoids distraction?

▪ Discover Distraction

Before you can deal with the distractions in your life, you will need to discover where and how you are being distracted. You will need to *identify your distractions*. This is a surprisingly useful and practical discipline. For

Christians living in a digital world, it is also a necessary one. If we wish to live with virtue in this strange new digital reality, we will need to reduce stimuli to focus on the few things that really matter.

Measure your use of media. You will need to spend time measuring the media in your life. This may well prove more difficult than you think. Studies show that when people are asked to report the amount of time they spend watching television, they chronically underreport it, often by several hours. Very few people think they watch four or five hours per day, and yet studies tell us that they do. So as you begin to find ways to destroy distraction in your life, seek to measure media by studying how you and the members of your family use it, how much you use it, and where you use it. Keep a log as you monitor television time, keep tabs on text messages sent and received, and watch how often the computer is accessed.

Find the beeps. Once you have measured the media in your life, you will need to find which media are particularly distracting for you. Try to intentionally notice when your devices buzz and beep and distract you, violating your time or space. Note any habits you have formed in your use of e-mail or text messaging, watching television, or using the Internet. Are you responding to work e-mails during time with your family? Are personal texts and e-mails taking time away from your work? Discover what is drawing you from one realm into another.

Find what dulls. Seek out those things that tend to dull your mind instead of sharpening it. Are there certain websites or media you use only when you are bored? Do you use them to dull your mind instead of sharpen it?

■ *Destroy Distraction*

Having searched for and having identified much of the distraction in your life, you will now need to take action to destroy and remove the distractions. Removing distraction may not be easy, but you will find that it frees your mind and heart to pursue better things.

Delete and unsubscribe. Begin to distance yourself from your distractions. Stop visiting particularly wasteful websites or put blocks on them so you can only visit them during certain times of the day. Unsubscribe from blogs that have no redeeming qualities. Be ruthless if necessary. You'll soon learn how much information you can live just fine without.

Focus on substance. You can't completely empty your mind. Nor would you want to. Instead, make sure you are filling it with thoughts that are useful, that contribute to the development of godly character and a life lived for God. Distractions will try to draw you down to shallow levels of thought and shallow ways of living. Eliminate distractions and fill your mind with ideas and thoughts that challenge you and increase your love for God.

▪ Cultivate Concentration

Our culture of distraction did not arise all at once. Rather, it came through time and practice. Yes, you practiced being distracted, and you managed to get better and better at it (congratulations!). Eventually you rewired your brain in such a way that it craves distraction and fights against concentration. The practice it took to become a distracted person proves that practice will be involved in *overcoming* distraction.

Focus. Develop particular interests and focus concentration on those few things. Dedicate more time to fewer things. Be very willing to let quality trump quantity.

Write. Write about what you learn. It may prove useful to write by hand—the old-fashioned way using old-fashioned tools. Buy a journal and record your thoughts there. Consider writing letters by hand. Writing on a computer allows you to write in short bursts, to rearrange rambling thoughts into some sort of eventually cohesive whole through the magic of copy and paste. Writing by hand requires greater focus because it demands a constant sense of what has already been said and what must still be said.

▪ Seek Solitude

As you identify and begin to destroy distraction, you will want to replace that distraction with solitude. This may not be the kind of solitude that requires a drive into the countryside or a weekend at a quiet cabin in the woods (though such times may be greatly beneficial). Instead, it calls for simple digital solitude, digital silence. Seek times and places that are far removed from the digital. Solitude can be intimidating for those who are accustomed to the beeps, to the hustle of digital living. Worse still, silence can seem boring, far less interesting than all the distraction we are sure we enjoy. Yet it is a practice Christians need to rediscover.

Take a digital fast. Set aside days in which you will fast from all digital media. On these days you will need to set aside your cell phone, turn off the television, put away the PlayStation, and leave the computer alone. The more difficult this sounds and the more difficult it proves to be, the more important it will be for you to do it.

Take a digital vacation. A day or two without digital media will be useful. But consider taking a break for an entire week or two. As you take time away from the home, office, or classroom, take time away from the digital. When you go on your next vacation, agree as a family to leave your devices behind, to refrain together from e-mail and cell phones, from text messages and Facebook. At the very least, turn off the ability for these devices to communicate (use your computer to browse the photographs you've been taking, but don't use it to surf the web).

Carve digital-free times. I have already noted a 2010 study that found that one-third of women between the ages of eighteen and thirty-four check Facebook when they first wake up, before they even head to the bathroom. Many more sleep with their cell phones at their side so they can immediately check text messages that may have come in overnight. Do not be in a hurry to begin your day with the digital. If you are in the habit of doing personal devotions in the morning, determine that you will not turn on your computer or look at your cell phone until you have read the Bible and spent time in prayer. When you have completed your work for the day, stay away from your computer until the children have gone to bed. I read recently of a family that has a "technology basket" in their home. When evening comes, they each take their most distracting piece of technology and place it in this basket, where it must remain for a few hours. Dad puts his cell phone in there, mom her Kindle, the kids their video games. This then frees the family to find other things to do, better things that bring them together instead of pushing them each into their private little worlds of media.

QUESTIONS FOR REFLECTION

1. How have the beeps in your life grown over the years? Do you feel that you are more or less distracted now than you were in the past? What would you identify as the main sources of your distraction?

2. Do you agree or disagree with the idea that distraction leads to shallow thinking and that shallow thinking leads to shallow living? Where do you see evidence of distraction that is causing shallow living in your life?

3. Do you have a device you find you just cannot live without? How do you feel when you leave home without it (if you can)? What is it about this device that keeps you so committed to it?

4. In what settings are you prone to multitasking? Have you found that you can do two or more things at once while maintaining high standards of quality in each area? What challenges and benefits does multitasking present?

5. Describe your typical reading habits. Do you find that you tend toward deeply engaging with a text as you read it? Or are you more prone to skimming? How have your habits changed over time?

ASIDE

Your Family and Media

No parent would ever put his child into the driver's seat of a car without first teaching him how to drive—without first showing him how to accelerate gently, brake properly, use the turn signals, react in an emergency. It is only when we have taught our children and mentored them that we allow them to set off on their own. Yet far too many parents are sending their children into an increasingly digital reality without proper training, without biblical instruction. If we want our children to use their technology well, if we want them to use it for God's glory, we need to be willing to teach and train them.

Here are seven steps to consider when it comes time to introduce new media, new technology, to your family.[1]

Educate. Before you can help your family use technology well, you will need to educate yourself (and by reading this book you've taken a good first step). As you introduce digital devices into your home, make sure you learn why your children want a device and what they intend to do with it. Research what their peers do with such devices—what they *actually* do with them. Think about what the device says it will do, but also how it might inadvertently influence your life. Do not be in a hurry to introduce devices, but take time to think about them with disciplined discernment.

Fence. Once you have introduced a new technology into your home, or decide that your child can now have access to it, you will need to erect fences and boundaries. Put boundaries around the time they dedicate to these devices (certain days of the week on which they may and may not use them; the number of minutes or hours on those days on which they use them) and put boundaries around the ways they use these devices—this may involve telling them which websites or how many text messages they may send).

Mentor. As your children begin to use these devices, watch them and mentor them to ensure they are using them well. Sit with your children as they use their new Facebook account, and watch them as they begin to explore the Internet. Instruct them, explaining what they are doing well and helping them when they make those inevitable bad decisions.

Supervise. Supervise your children as they use their devices. Do not give your children full and unlimited access to the Internet, and do not give them computers they can use behind the privacy of closed doors. Instead, keep the computer in a public place, and let them know that all of their use should be considered public. Explore some of the hardware and software solutions available to parents to filter out inappropriate content. Let your children know that using cell phones and computers are privileges that fall under your jurisdiction.

Review. As your children use their technologies, ask them what they've done through their devices. It is a good idea to find reports of what they have done — what they have looked at, what they have read and said. Many filters and other parental controls will alert you of inappropriate use.

Trust. As your children grow, give them more trust and express greater confidence in them. As they mature, they will grow in their ability to use their technologies well and will earn a greater measure of your trust.

Model. While you instruct your children, be careful to model disciplined discernment in your own use of technology. Your lessons will fall flat if you are searching for inappropriate content or if you are addicted to your cell phone. Model restraint and ownership of your devices.

CHAPTER 7

MORE
is
BETTER
(Information)

Dr. Edward Hallowell, psychiatrist and longtime faculty member at Harvard Medical School, is recognized as one of the world's foremost experts on attention-deficit/hyperactivity disorder. After years of studying and treating ADHD, Hallowell began to note a similar disorder, one that had stark similarities to ADHD with one notable exception—this is a condition his patients were inadvertently imposing on themselves. He termed this condition *attention deficit trait*.

ADT is a product of the digital world, a result of our obsession with information—our desire to surround ourselves with it, with *more* of it, all the time. In an interview with CNET News, Hallowell observed, "It's a condition induced by modern life, in which you've become so busy attending to so many inputs and outputs that you become increasingly distracted, irritable, impulsive, restless, and, over the long term, underachieving." People will know they've succumbed to it "when they start answering questions in ways that are more superficial, more hurried, than they usually would; when their reservoir of new ideas starts to run dry;

when they find themselves working ever-longer hours and sleeping less, exercising less, spending free time with friends less, and in general putting in more hours but getting less production overall." In other words, they will know they've got it when they find that they no longer have time or ability to give to building relationships or to fulfilling their God-given mandate that they work, create, innovate.

Arising as a direct result of overloading the brain's internal circuitry with too much input, ADT carries significant consequences. Hallowell states, "Aside from underachievement, you don't ever get the fulfillment of seeing yourself coming up with the ideas you ought to come up with. You don't get the fulfillment that comes from creative activity. You live at a much more surface level."[1]

I don't anticipate that attention deficit trait will ever be recognized as an official disorder, and I'm sure it is better this way. But the term is helpful in giving a name to a phenomenon many of us experience—a phenomenon caused by the digital explosion. The result of all of these new kinds of input, all of these sources of information, is that we live at a surface level. Our minds are too scattered to think in a focused direction, too drawn to the mundane to endure times of sustained reflection. Amid all of our information, we have little time for wisdom. We have little time, little ability, to heed Paul's admonition: "Brothers, do not be children in your thinking. Be infants in evil, but in your thinking be mature" (1 Corinthians 14:20). We cannot grow in our thinking, we cannot mature, if we cannot think at all.

Information Is Not Enough

The Christian life is one that is spent in the constant pursuit of wisdom, for it is wisdom that allows us to live in a distinctly Christian way. In Proverbs, Solomon personifies wisdom, describing her as a woman who stands at the street corners and city gates and invites men to come and learn from her. "Hear, for I will speak noble things, and from my lips will come what is right, for my mouth will utter truth; wickedness is an abomination to my lips" (Proverbs 8:6–7). The starting point for all that the Bible knows as wisdom is the knowledge of God. "The fear of the LORD is the beginning of wisdom, and the knowledge of the Holy One is insight" (Proverbs 9:10). This is the principle that controls all of Proverbs—that to know wisdom, one must first know the Lord.

In the New Testament, we find a similar emphasis on wisdom from James, who writes, "If any of you lacks wisdom, let him ask God, who gives generously to all without reproach, and it will be given him" (James 1:5). Wisdom, the Scriptures tell us, is the foundation of right living, the way in which God instructs us to live in the world for his glory.

We hear little about wisdom today. Instead, we hear more and more about the importance of *information*—about the virtues of information and the benefits of *more* information. But it is important to recognize that information and wisdom are not the same thing. In the 1980s, Russell Ackoff, longtime professor at Wharton School of the University of Pennsylvania, popularized what has since become known as the DIKW model, a model that aptly marks the progression from data to wisdom. Ackoff suggested the following progression:

Data —> Information —> Knowledge —> Wisdom

At the most basic level, we have *data*, which simply describes one or more symbols. A letter, an emoticon, a list of numbers within a spreadsheet—these are all *data*. They represent raw symbols and have no meaning outside of their context.

As we collect data into a kind of cohesive whole we create *information*. Information answers basic questions about the data: the *who, what, where,* and *when?* Information is data that has been assigned some kind of relational connection or has some kind of meaning. If we add a heading to a list of numbers in a spreadsheet, we have made data into information; we have turned a list of numbers into a list of prices or ages or totals. We now know what these pieces of data are meant to represent.

When we collect, collate, and compare pieces of information, we have acquired *knowledge*. Knowledge makes information useful. A multiplication table is an example of knowledge, a table we can memorize that allows us to use information in a useful way so that we can always know that 2 times 2 equals 4 and 9 times 9 equals 81. Solomon's proverbs, the hundreds of them listed from chapters 10 to 29 of his book—if we simply commit them to memory—are a form of knowledge. Knowledge is a "general awareness or possession of information, facts, ideas, truths, or principles."[2]

Finally, when we use knowledge to make good decisions, when we apply facts and knowledge to life situations, we express *wisdom*. Wisdom combines knowledge with experience to live with virtue. Every day we encounter data, information, and knowledge, yet God calls us to live with *wisdom*.

The poet T. S. Eliot once noted that information was subservient to knowledge and wisdom, asking in poetic form:

Where is the Life we have lost in living?
Where is the wisdom we have lost in knowledge?
Where is the knowledge we have lost in information?[3]

In this digital age, wisdom and even knowledge are often downplayed in favor of information. Information, available in unprecedented quantities, is no longer seen as a means to a higher and nobler end, a tool by which we increase our knowledge so we might live with wisdom. Instead, information has become an end in itself. We have begun to believe that the accumulation of information somehow leads to wisdom, that more information will solve society's ills and improve our lives. We place our faith in information. In our hearts and minds, having more data and more information will necessarily lead to progress.

In the last chapter, we looked at the growing problem of distraction. We saw how digital living has created many new means of distraction and has re-created us in the image of distraction. And here, as we begin to understand our dedication to information, we see how information and distraction are closely connected. The fact is that we may actually *want* to be interrupted, because each interruption brings a new bit of information.[4] Every e-mail brings a nugget of news, every text message a word from a friend. In both cases, they bring us information, and if information is inherently good, inherently desirable, of course we are glad to be interrupted, to be distracted by it. We need our distraction in order to further our commitment to information. We need a constant flow of information, even if it means interrupting what we are doing, whether sitting in the office or the church pew. When we are disconnected from our sources of information, we feel as though we are disconnected from the world, as if life will move on without us. We find joy and life in that information—not in using that information or turning that information into useful action, but simply in its constant flow.

Glut

For most of human history, information was a scarce resource. When we read of the men and women of biblical times, we should keep in mind that they were people who had access to only very small amounts of information. In an entire lifetime, they would encounter less information than you or I can store in our mobile phones. It was not until the invention of the printing press that we transitioned from a world of information scarcity into a world of information abundance. This groundbreaking technology allowed books to be printed so cheaply that a literate person of moderate means could easily collect more books than he could ever read. Even the person who read hundreds or thousands of books in a lifetime had access to hundreds and thousands more that he simply could not read.

Yet because there were fixed costs associated with publishing books, only a small percentage of the total potential books were ever printed. A publisher assumed all of the risk in producing a book, investing time in having it typeset and paying printing costs before he could sell even a single copy and begin to recoup his expenses. For this reason, the publisher represented an initial filter. He did not just print the book, but he also decided whether it would be published in the first place. Booksellers represented a second level of filtering, choosing to dedicate shelf space to some books and not to others. And, of course, consumers filtered books as well, choosing to purchase titles related to subjects that interested them and by authors who inspired them. Even while there was an abundance of information available through books, filters were naturally created that allowed people to deal effectively with such abundance.[5]

Times have changed. Today any of us has the power to publish. If we want to share a book with the world, we can turn to any one of the myriad self-publishing companies and within days have a copy of our own book in hand. But even easier, any of us can start a blog to discuss our hobbies, open a Facebook account to tell about our lives, and head to Flickr to share our photographs. And most of us are doing at least some of these things. There are no filters here (which you know if you have ever read a MySpace blog) — no publishers who take it upon themselves to decide what can be published and what cannot.

This has led to far more than information abundance; it has led to information glut. The filters are gone, and we are gorging ourselves on information. Even in times of information scarcity, people often had more information at their disposal than they could ever use in a meaningful way. Today access has increased exponentially. The amount of digital data created by the end of 2010 surpassed a zettabyte, an amount that almost defies explanation (think of 75 billion iPads stuffed to capacity). By the year 2020, this amount is expected to increase by a factor of 44 (this gets just plain silly after a while, but imagine a stack of DVDs, each full of data, reaching halfway to Mars).[6]

This glut of data has many causes, though for sake of convenience we can divide them into two categories: (1) our digital technology creates it, and (2) our ideology demands it.

▪ Why All This Glut?

In the first place, this glut is a necessary consequence of our digital advances. Through our new technologies:

- there is more information being created by more people than ever before.
- vast amounts of old information are being digitized (such as Google's attempt to digitize and catalog every book ever written).
- we have witnessed quantum leaps forward in the ability to duplicate and transmit information — and so the information is not just in existence but is also accessible to us.
- information is available through more channels than ever before. It comes to us through the old media of radio and television and newspapers, but it also pours in through the new media of Facebook and Twitter, blogs and text messages, websites and e-readers.

No wonder, then, that we hear more and more today about information overload. No wonder that we feel overwhelmed at times, as if we are drowning in a torrent of facts and figures, words and pictures, messages and videos, text messages and e-mails. This is not far from the truth. Though the vast majority of the zettabyte of information exists in databases and is relevant only to computers, you and I still face far more information than people have ever had to sort through in the past. Many of us are crumbling under the pressure of it, struggling to deal with the unending deluge.

Our technologies create the data glut, but this is not all; our ideologies also demand it. Quentin Schultze, professor of communication arts and sciences at Calvin College, observes the godlike importance we attach to information and coins the word *informationism* to describe it. According to Schultze, informationism is "a non-discerning, vacuous faith in the collection and dissemination of information as a route to social progress and personal happiness." Rising nearly to the realm of religion, informationism preaches "the *is* over the *ought*, *observation* over *intimacy*, and *measurement* over *meaning*."[7] This is to say that information becomes ultimate; it becomes the lens through which we understand life, through which we understand ourselves.

What is new in the aftermath of the digital explosion is not the fact that we like information or that we desire it. What is unique to our time and our technological context is our near-total dedication to it, our belief in its inherent goodness. As we have transitioned from information scarcity to a time of information abundance and even information overload, the challenge is not in gathering the information but in knowing what to do with it, in piecing together some sort of meaning from it, some knowledge, some wisdom. What we are finding is that more information does not necessarily lead to more wisdom. In fact, the very opposite may be true.

More information may lead to *less* wisdom.

■ Information Overload

Torkel Klingberg, professor of cognitive neuroscience at Karolinska Institute in Sweden, recently performed a study of information overload and the limits of working memory. He concluded that the sheer volume of information we encounter is causing us to bump up against limitations within our brains. This is not to say that our brains will not or cannot adapt in order to deal with new realities. After all, the brain is remarkably plastic and able to adapt if and when necessary. However, such adaptation takes time. For the time being, we have print-age brains in a digital world, and in many ways we are overtaxing them with too much stimulus, too much information. Klingberg observes, "The demands of the information society, with its copious information, simultaneous situations, pace, and distractions, make many of us feel as though we are suffering from some sort of attention deficit."[8]

While we may not have read the studies proving this, most of us already feel it. We know why cell phone usage leads to a higher incidence of traffic accidents—we simply cannot deal adequately with all of the information at once. Our attention is drawn this way and that and hopefully, at least sometimes, back again. And even when we do begin to adapt to our technology, its pace increases. It is very likely that you are 10 percent better at talking on the phone while processing e-mail than you were a few years ago. But all the while, the number of e-mails you receive per day has probably increased by 200 percent. Thus, even while your abilities grow, so too does your need to develop new abilities.[9] "We have reached a point," writes John Naish, "where our lives are logjammed with junk data. I don't just mean illegal spam but also the time-robbing, nourishment-free information that we lay on each other every day through e-mails, phone calls, and texts."[10]

This is not to say that we've proven helpless in the face of all this information. As we have taken great strides forward in creating and accessing information, we have also taken steps forward in filtering it. Data mining allows us to look through seemingly unrelated data to find patterns; it allows us to programmatically create information from mere data. Search engines, following the lead of Google, allow us to filter the few relevant pieces of information from the billions of irrelevant. Think back to the first generation of search engines, compare them to the ones that exist today, and you'll have to acknowledge the contrast.

And yet we still feel overwhelmed. As if to prove a point about technology, many of us turn to digital technologies to solve the problems digital technology has caused. (Just as our governments create debt in order to solve debt, we create technology to solve technology. It's foolproof!) We try new devices that can access all of our information from a single point, or we try new software that can do a better job of filtering the good from the bad, the very good from the mere average. We trust in computers and algorithms. But in the end we just have too much information coming our way, too many entry points for it, and too little ability to cope with it. Klingberg writes:

> Our relationship to information is ambivalent. We clearly often seek out more, quicker, and more complex information, as if we're getting a kick from the shot. But when we're sitting on the sofa trying to read the on-screen text while trying to follow the headlines, many of us are struck with a feeling of inadequacy, with a sense that our brain is already full of information. It's overflowing.[11]

Combine the amount and accessibility of information with strides in filtering it, and we see that the flow of information has been engineered toward greater and greater efficiency. Yet much work remains. Even the best tools are still frustratingly poor and tend to create problems of their own, even while they seek to solve another problem (remember that every technology has both benefits and drawbacks). Google allows us to search widely, searching across websites, news reports, books, images, videos, and social media. Yet a return of 10 million results hardly helps us as we seek to get out from underneath the information available to us. Neither are we necessarily assisted by a return of only snippets of information, all of which is surrounded by more information in the form of advertising.

My concern with information overload is not so much that it will keep you from doing your job, that in your workplace you will find yourself overwhelmed with a deluge of information and be unable to get your work done; my concern is that as we dedicate ourselves to the pursuit of more information from more sources, we will be so overloaded by information that we will no longer have the time—perhaps even the ability—to ponder that information, to consider it, to take the time to study it and analyze it and meditate on it.

Knowledge versus Access

In his five-part trilogy *The Hitchhiker's Guide to the Galaxy*—which I, like everyone else my age, read during my college years—Douglas Adams writes about a resource called the *Encyclopedia Galactica* and its competition *The Hitchhiker's Guide to the Galaxy* (which, though wildly inaccurate, is more popular because it is slightly cheaper and on the cover cheerily warns "DON'T PANIC"). Each book lays claim to being the standard repository of all of the world's knowledge. The *Guide* is composed of entries of varied quality, some of which are lengthy and accurate, while others are short and contain unfortunate errors (such as the entry for the "Ravenous Bugblatter Beasts" for which the entry states that "Ravenous Bugblatter Beasts often make a very good meal *for* visiting tourists" rather than the more accurate "Ravenous Bugblatter Beasts often make a very good meal *of* visiting tourists.").[12] Some of the entries are written by staff members and experts, while others are written by anyone who happens to wander by the office and feels inspired to write. It is also far from objective at times, and nasty and sarcastic at other times. I am not the first to note its similarity to Wikipedia and, perhaps more so, to the Internet in general. Such a guide, a repository to all information, all knowledge, has long been a dream of humans. And it is starting to come true. Today we have more sources of information and knowledge than ever before, and we have more ways of accessing them.

During my aforementioned weeklong digital fast, I quickly became aware of how accustomed I am to having instant information on any subject that enters my mind. Driving through a small Maryland town, I saw a truck that was advertising farrier services. I thought I knew what a farrier did but felt the urge to look it up to be sure. I saw a license plate in New York that read "The Empire State" and immediately felt compelled to find out how New York earned that slogan. In both cases, I resisted only because of my desire to stay digital free for the week. There was no real purpose to seeking such information; I just wanted to know it, and I would have found out if I hadn't sworn off technology at that time.

Information comes to us far more easily now than at any other time in history. We grow closer to the *Encyclopedia Galactica*. As a digital immigrant, I grew up in what today feels like the dark ages. These were the days before computerized catalogs. When I went to the library to find resources for a research project, I had to look in a massive wooden card catalog to find books on my subject. The primary means of discovering information was to find a good book, to look in its bibliography, and from there to seek to find the titles this book had relied on. The libraries had no relational databases then, no way of easily searching across an entire library for books on a similar subject or by the same author.

Today, of course, I can use my iPhone to access the library's catalog across the Internet and in a matter of seconds find any number of books and have the library reserve them for me. Or I can order them from Amazon and have them show up tomorrow. Or I can go on Google Books and read at least a portion of each. I can find so much information that I may not even need books—at least books of the printed, physical variety. It used to be that research was a slow and painstaking task. Today it is as easy as an Internet search.

Information is at our fingertips all the time. We access it habitually, constantly. But we also access it lightly. Our access to information is a mile wide, but our knowledge is just an inch deep. This digital world has given us an obsession with accessing; indeed, it has raised accessing information to the level of a virtue. And it has done so at the expense of knowledge. It has given us plenty of knowledge *about* but little knowledge *of.*

This distinction between knowledge of and knowledge about is a critical one. Let me illustrate with a few words about my favorite person. I know a lot *about* my wife. I know what she likes to wear around the house, what she likes to wear to church, and what she likes to wear when we go out for dinner. I know what she likes to eat and what she hates to eat. I know what books she likes to read, what movies she likes to watch, what websites she likes to browse. I have all of this accumulated knowledge about my wife. But I think I could have this same level of knowledge about whomever the latest Hollywood heartthrob happens to be. This is exactly the kind of knowledge I can find in the newspapers and magazines that clutter the checkouts at the grocery store, and it is the kind of knowledge I can find on the hundreds of gossip blogs that pollute the Internet. It is not the kind of knowledge that will necessarily make me a good husband, one who serves my wife well.

I also have knowledge *of* my wife, knowledge that goes far beyond the facts of preferences, likes, dislikes, and hobbies. I have an intense and intimate knowledge of my wife — a kind of knowledge shared by no one else in the world. She and I enjoy intimacy that transcends mere bits of information. I know who she is behind closed doors; I know who she is at both her best moments and her worst; I know things about her that no one else could ever know. I know her and am known by her with a depth that is unique to the marriage relationship. And isn't this the true virtue in knowing? Don't we all want to know intimately and to be known intimately?

A trend we see today through our digital technologies is the *exaltation of knowledge about*, a kind of knowledge composed of cold facts. This comes at the expense of a more intimate kind of knowledge. Quentin Schultze states that we have become like tourists who are so enamored by our mode of transportation that we cruise through nation after nation largely indifferent to the people and the cultures around us.[13] We have our passports filled with the little stamps telling everyone just how many places we've been, but we don't stop to ask what the purpose is of traveling the nations if we have not actually *experienced* them. And what is the purpose of knowing people if we do not care to know them on anything more than a surface level?

We see this in a technology like Facebook or Twitter. Social media provide a conduit for endless knowledge of facts about the lives of our friends and families. We can log on and at any time see what our friends are doing at that moment and what they have done, update by update, since they first joined; we can see who their friends are, what movies they enjoy, what books they read (or don't read), what blogs they like, where they were born, what networks and groups they belong to, and on and on. We learn all of this information about them, even if we do not know them. These facts bring us no closer to knowledge of them — of who they really are. We have hundreds of people flitting around on the edges of our lives, but perhaps fewer than ever with whom we are intimately involved.

This trend manifests itself in other ways. We are increasingly moving knowledge to the "cloud" and relying on knowledge that exists in the "cloud." The *cloud*, of course, is that sum of data and information that exists "out there." When you need to know what is in that bottle of pills you left in the closet and type its name into Google, you are accessing the cloud. It is convenient, to be sure. But it trains us in the skill of *accessing information* instead of teaching us what is really valuable to know and understand. We are becoming people who have access to vast amounts of knowledge with a few taps of our thumbs but who retain just little bits of knowledge in our minds and hearts.

This leads us to care more about accessing information that will make our lives immediately easier, that will fix our little problems, than to carefully and thoughtfully consider the morality of what we do with that information. The information we access is seen as having no moral purpose. It is purely practical. I need to know the lyrics for this song, but I am not concerned about the fact that I have downloaded it illegally. This mind-set allows us to manipulate the world so we can get what we want when we want it.

Students increasingly see study, not as a means of acquiring knowledge that will impact their lives and benefit society, but as a means to getting good grades and making parents and teachers happy. So we download essays from the Internet, caring nothing of the morality of doing so or of the missed opportunity to actually learn something. Quentin Schulze says of this new world, "To know is to leverage information to accomplish instrumental goals."[14] Heart knowledge is downplayed in favor of using information to get what we want, now. It's immediate, but it's fleeting.

Our devices are unparalleled in their ability to give us access to this information anytime and anywhere. There is no evil inherent in this. One of the great benefits of the information age, ironically, is that it allows us to know less because we can look up anything at a click of the mouse.[15] We can access information that would otherwise reside in only a few minds. We are grateful for this when we encounter poison ivy and want to find a way of dealing with the itch. But it is a benefit that can have diminishing returns.

As we increasingly dedicate ourselves to the pursuit of information, we grow increasingly unable or unwilling to distinguish between knowledge and information, wisdom and knowledge. We do well to ask: If we have little knowledge in our minds, how much can we have in our hearts?

Memory

I've hinted at another possible problem with the ease of access to information. What we have in our minds is not the same as what we can access through a computer. Memories stored electronically are not the same as those stored in our minds and hearts. Let's consider two key ideas here: (1) the outsourcing of memory from the human brain to the form of bits and bytes, and (2) the eternality of information.

▪ Outsourcing of Memory

A genuine benefit of the information age is that we can now know less than ever before. We don't have to know everything; we just need to know where and how to find it. This comes in handy when one of our children gets stung by a bee. Instead of relying on memory, we can simply do a search and find ways to treat it. But this is a benefit that can have diminishing returns. Eventually we may prefer to outsource more of our memories, leaving less in our brains. And this may be subtly influencing the way we value the ability to remember things. We are beginning to see electronic memory as superior to organic memory, believing in some way that the hard drive is better than the brain.

Because of the ease, low cost, and convenience of online storage, we are increasingly outsourcing our memories, putting online what would otherwise require effort to remember. Over the years, the Net has transitioned from being a supplement to personal memory to being a replacement for personal memory. Today we talk about artificial memory as if it is indistinguishable from biological memory, as if remembering in my mind and remembering by searching my blog is inherently equal.[16] Suddenly those old feats of memory, those old spiritual disciplines, seem dated, unnecessary. What use is there in memorizing Scripture if I can access my favorite translation (and hundreds of others) faster than I can begin to recite it? Why expend effort in getting the Bible into my heart and mind if I already have it in my pocket?

Beginning with the invention of writing and on to the more recent development of photography, memory has become externalized to varying degrees. We wrote in books what we wanted to remember without having to force it into our brains, and we took photographs to record our most important moments. And yet we did not consider these in any way *better* than personal memory; we considered them supplemental at best.

It is only through our recent digital advances that we've been able to record massive quantities of information with only the slightest bit of work (or sometimes with no work at all) and with a sense that this information will be preserved safely and permanently. We can snap hundreds of photos, thousands of them, and make only the tiniest dent in our storage space. We can write billions of words and not even come close to filling the smallest hard drive. Along the way, we've started to understand the brain as a kind of hard drive; we've reduced the differences between the human brain and the computer. If they are essentially two manifestations of the same thing, it makes sense to take as much out of the brain as possible. This allows us to free up processing capacity and storage capacity and allows us to store it all in something safer and less prone to corruption than the human gray matter.

But there is a danger here. "Those who celebrate the 'outsourcing' of memory to the web have been misled by a metaphor. They overlook the fundamentally organic nature of biological memory. What gives real memory its richness and its character, not to mention its mystery and fragility, is its contingency. It exists in time, changing as the body changes."[17] Where a computer takes in information and immediately stores it as data, the human brain continues to process that information and turn it into a form of knowledge. Biological memory is a living memory; computer memory is not.

What is committed to memory, what is installed there through the labor of memorization, is of special significance. We commit Scripture to memory, not as a functional habit, but because the discipline of memorizing it forces us to meditate on it and allows us to call it to mind at any time. Putting it into our brains aids us as we seek to put it into our hearts, understand it in a more holistic sense than mere data, and then live it out through our lives. We commit favorite poems to memory because we can then recall them at opportune times as we revel in their beauty. We stare at our loved ones, memorizing their features, noticing the little details, building a picture of them in our minds and in our memories.

But as we outsource our brains to digital media, we threaten our ability to make information into knowledge and knowledge into wisdom. We train ourselves, not to remember, but to forget. Empty minds will beget empty hearts and empty lives.

▪ Eternality of Information

Remembering has always been both time-consuming and costly. In ancient days, remembering involved a great deal of effort in committing facts to memory or committing them and then preserving them on some kind of a medium. If I wanted to remember what I did over the course of a day, week, or month, I would need to record events in a journal, invest time and effort in maintaining it, and then keep the journal safe. Almost inevitably, it would in time get damaged or destroyed, and those memories would be lost forever. With the dawn of digital technologies and the massive cost decreases in storage, it has become more difficult to forget than to remember. And the number of collection points has risen dramatically. Everything I've ever said or done on Facebook is recorded there forever; every search I've made on Google or Yahoo is there somewhere. It exists in digital memory.

The Internet Archive is a nonprofit organization that exists to ensure that what happens on the Internet is preserved. The site's founders mean to protect society's right to know and right to remember all that has happened online. To that end they take regular snapshots of websites and archive them in a kind of digital time capsule that any Internet user can access. And so we can all look to the past to see what we said and did all those years ago. I can look to the earliest days of my website and see the embarrassing things I wrote there, long before I understood that it was a public website. And you can visit sites where you posted comments and see the silly or irrational things you posted as well. It's all there, just waiting to be discovered, waiting to be recalled from the archives.

While we put online what we wish to remember, we also put online what we might otherwise forget. Knowledge has always equaled power. We have always held back knowledge about ourselves from others in order to maintain power. We release knowledge of ourselves, especially intimate knowledge, only with great hesitation. We tell deep secrets only to the closest of our friends and leave much, both sinful and honorable, between God and ourselves. We deliberately forget because forgetting is a blessing, on both an emotional level and a spiritual level. Forgetting is a natural part of the human experience and a natural function of the human brain. It is a feature, not a bug—one that saves us from being owned by our memories.

During the days of Communism in the Soviet Union, the KGB would stamp "to be preserved forever" on the dossiers of its political prisoners. The message was clear: the state did not and would not forget those who had betrayed her. And this shaped the people. It had to! They knew that what they had done in the past would always be held against them and at any moment could be used in prosecuting them. This is the message of our data today. What we say, what we do, the people we communicate with, the things we search for, the places we go—they are all stamped with "to be preserved forever." Our data never goes away. We can never change, never put on a new skin. What we said twenty years ago is preserved alongside what we said this morning.

I love biographies. I love to read about the great men and women of days past, to learn how ordinary people became extraordinary. Like most people, I particularly enjoy reading the biographies of those who have long since died. After a person dies, there are few surprises. Once a person has died, there is no longer any question of whether he will forsake his faith at the end of his life or fall into a particular sin. When he dies, the record is closed. Very often, biographies rely on journals, correspondence, and other documents that, during the person's life, remained secret. These documents provide a view deep into a person's heart. There is not much we will not confess to our journals. Yet there is even more we will confess to our search engines. We reconstruct the most intimate parts of a person's life from his search history. What does your search history say about you? What will it say if, fifty years from now, all search information data becomes public domain? It may not tell about things that are perverse and dark, but it may well tell of things that are personal and humiliating.

Through the long history of humanity, forgetting has been normal, and remembering has been the exception. But with today's digital technologies, the balance has shifted so that remembering is the default, and forgetting is the great exception.[18] And can a world that never forgets be a world that truly forgives? Author Viktor Mayer-Schönberger asks, "If all our past activities, transgressions or not, are always present, how can we disentangle ourselves from them in our thinking and decision making? Might perfect remembering make us as unforgiving to ourselves as to others?"[19]

While the search engines may never forget, while those who capture data about us may never forget, we serve a God who *does* forget and who places great emphasis on the virtue of forgetting. He accepts all those who turn to him and confess their sins. Psalm 103:12 promises, "As far as the east is from the west, so far does he remove our transgressions from us." In Hebrews 8:12, God makes this promise: "I will be merciful toward their iniquities, and I will remember their sins no more." And in these things he commands us to imitate him — to forgive all offenses and to never again bring those sins to mind.

How can we forgive if we can never forget? How can we move beyond a sinful past if we know that the evidence of it lives on somewhere, waiting to be mined, waiting to be discovered? Can we leave a past transgression between ourselves and God, knowing that the evidence of us remains in a database and may someday be drawn out?

Even today, when Facebook will remember every old boyfriend, every bad photograph and unkind word, every foolish sin of our younger days, we must be willing and eager to forgive as we've been forgiven, to forget as God has forgotten our transgressions against him.

Outside the Torrent

Information is an asset; it is a tool, but it is no more than that. Information is not virtuous; it is not an end in itself. If we are to live virtuous lives in the aftermath of this digital explosion, we must learn to deal with unending sources of information, and how to survive amid its constant flow. As we deal with increasing levels of information, we have to develop skills to distinguish between what is important and what is mundane.

We are becoming a people whose knowledge is a mile wide and an inch deep. The Bible seems to tell us that it would be far better to know fewer things, but to know those things on a much deeper level. Virtue is not in the accumulation of facts, in winning a game on *Jeopardy*, but in living a life marked by wisdom, by the application of knowledge. If we are to live in this way, we must be willing to step outside the torrent of information; we must be willing to understand that information is a great servant but a lousy master.

APPLICATION
Growing in Wisdom

As Christians, it is imperative that we live in ways that are marked with wisdom born of deep knowledge. Our *theology* tells us that we must live distinctly Christian lives, lives marked by God's wisdom. And in order to do this, we must have knowledge of who God is and what he requires of us.

Our experience tells us that we are prone to lose knowledge in the midst of all of the data and information that surrounds us. Our increasing distractions, our growing number of stimuli, keep us from being able to ponder information, to take what we know and have it inform how we live.

And our theory of technology informs us that amid all of the opportunity that comes to us through the many new sources of information, we also bear an associated risk—that the very information we love will overwhelm us.

How can we live in the sweet spot between them?

Get wisdom. In a culture obsessed with information, we have found that more information does not necessarily mean we will have any more knowledge or wisdom. In fact, the very opposite may be true. It may well be that less information will lead to greater wisdom. Without the distraction of dealing with vast amounts of information and without overtaxing our brains with hundreds of sources of information, we will have the time to know more about less. "The beginning of wisdom is this: Get wisdom, and whatever you get, get insight" (Proverbs 4:7). Above all else, know and understand the difference between information, knowledge, and wisdom, and always seek information that can be turned into useful knowledge and wisdom to live by.

Measure input. We have already sought to measure our media, but here we want to measure our information—a difficult thing to do. But you can begin by focusing for just a day or two on the sources of information in your life. It will include television and newspaper, radio and blogs, Facebook and text messages. Try to quantify the information that comes your way; seek to understand how much of it serves a tangible purpose and how much of it is really just noise.

Choose quality over quantity. Once you understand that more information does not necessarily lead to a better life, you will want to begin to reduce the sources of input in your life. First consider which sources deliver to you the best, most valuable sources of information, and then consider which deliver the worst, least valuable sources of information. Cut out those ones. Emphasize quality over quantity. If you find that some of your Facebook friends only distract you through posting mindless links or vapid updates, hide them or de-friend them. If there are blogs that you sort through even though they bring no benefit, unsubscribe to them.

Simplify. Our intellectual technologies always bring costs alongside the benefits. And we seem hard-wired to assume that within the technologies that caused the problems lies the solution—that technology can solve the problems caused by technology. We complicate rather than simplify. As you consider reducing your sources of information, consider nontechnical solutions. Consider moving backward instead of forward.

Memorize. Memorization is a dying virtue today. When it is so easy to store information and to access information, there seems to be little virtue in memorizing. Yet Christians have long maintained that there is great benefit in memorizing Scripture, since the very process moves God's words from our minds to our hearts to our lives. Not only that, but once Scripture is in our minds, we can continually ruminate on it, allowing it to shape and mold us. There is no digital equivalent to the benefit brought about by memorizing the Word of God.

Make it count. Try to increasingly access only the information you actually need—information that will be of real benefit to your life, to your faith. And seek to move that information to knowledge and to wisdom. Make every bit of information you access count.

QUESTIONS FOR REFLECTION

1. Dr. Hallowell says that attention deficit trait leaves a person dry for good ideas, working longer hours with less to show for it, spending less time with friends and family, putting in more time but seeing less production. In what ways do you feel that you struggle with "attention deficit"? Does this trait describe your life?

2. T. S. Eliot asked where the knowledge is that we have lost in information. When do you feel most overloaded by information? What is the danger in all of this? How might having more information actually lead to less wisdom?

3. Amid all of the information available today, it is easy to believe that *access* to information is as virtuous as real knowledge. What do you see as the difference between these two? How might this be a danger when we relate to Scripture and God's truth?

4. How have you "outsourced" your memory, relying on digital storage for information you need? What is the value of this technology? What do you see as a potential danger?

CHAPTER 8

HERE COMES EVERYBODY (Truth/Authority)

When I was a boy, I always wanted my parents to buy the *Encyclopedia Britannica*. I was that kind of a kid, I suppose. At least once a year, a salesman would knock at the door and give us an opportunity to buy the complete set. We *had* to act quickly because it was not available in stores (that's what we were told). It was an amazing offer, the best and most complete source of compiled knowledge available, the Cadillac of encyclopedia sets.

First published as three volumes in 1768, the *Britannica* grew into a massive set of thirty-two hardbound volumes jam-packed with knowledge. Overseen by a staff of over a hundred full-time editors and drawing on the expertise of 4,000 expert contributors, it was the closest I could come to knowing a little bit about everything and learning it from an authoritative source. Unfortunately, the cost was prohibitive. We never did buy it.

The encyclopedia salesman is now a quaint vestige of days gone by, and the encyclopedia itself, at least in its traditional form, does not seem far behind. There is little place for the *Britannica* in an Internet world. Jump onto

Google, search for *britannica*—and the first result will take you to the site of the *Encyclopedia*; the second, rather ironically, will take you to Wikipedia.

Wikipedia is the brainchild of Jimmy Wales and Larry Sanger. Launched in January 2001, it added to the concept of the encyclopedia, a repository of knowledge, the ground-shaking idea of allowing anyone to add to and edit its content (an idea now known by the strange moniker *wiki*). By the end of that year, it featured nearly 20,000 articles; by 2009, it exceeded 15 million articles spread across 240 languages (3 million of them were in English). Only recently has its growth shown signs of leveling off. Wikipedia consistently ranks near the top of the most-read sites on the Internet and attracts around 75 million visitors per month. The site for *Encyclopedia Britannica* receives less than 2 percent of that total.

Encyclopedia Britannica stands as a pillar of the old world, the print world. Though still available in printed format, its end is likely near. Wikipedia stands as a pillar of the new world, the digital world. It continues to grow and thrive. Though both are repositories of knowledge, there is a world of difference between them.

Britannica offers 65,000 articles totaling some 44 million words. Each article is written by one of 4,000 experts and is passed through an editorial process that ensures quality and accuracy. They offer the assurance that all of the information is not only correct but also authoritative. This promise holds weight because the articles are written by *experts* in their fields— Arnold Palmer wrote the article for the Master's tournament; professional skateboarder Tony Hawk wrote the article on skateboarding. They boast that they have the most Nobel Prize winners of any encyclopedia and that they employ an army of fact-checkers who constantly work through the articles to ensure that they are accurate and up-to-date. An updated edition appears every few years with an annual Yearbook providing updated coverage of the previous years' events.

Wikipedia offers 15 million articles and a word count that must extend into the billions. There are nearly 13 million registered users, each of whom has the ability to add new articles or edit existing ones. Wikipedia takes the view that by democratizing the creation of content, they can have far more than 4,000 experts involved who can fact-check, who can verify both quality and accuracy. If I notice a typo, I can immediately edit it on my own; if I notice a fact I disagree with, I can immediately change it (and so, too, can my ten-year old son). Experts or those with academic credentials are given no extra weight or authority. Wikipedia is in a state of constant flux, with many articles being edited on a daily basis.

Of course, an encyclopedia is only as good as the accuracy of the information it contains, and there have been many debates about the accuracy of the traditional model versus the wiki model.* A 2005 study by *Nature* found that articles from Wikipedia averaged four errors each, while articles from *Britannica* averaged three errors (though in both cases what constituted an error was sometimes suspect).[1] The editors of *Encyclopedia Britannica* protested the results, insisting that their product is far more accurate than they were given credit for. Reading their evidence, it is difficult to disagree. One interesting aspect was the study's findings about the fluidity of the articles on Wikipedia. Each article maintains a complete history, and a search of this history will often show hundreds, sometimes thousands or tens of thousands, of changes along the way. Pages are vandalized and restored; cliques develop as facts are disputed. A page is constantly in flux as "facts" are changed this way and that; the article today may be very different from the article yesterday. Eventually, if there are too many changes or if there is too much controversy about certain facts, Wikipedia may lock down the page and allow changes to be made only by authorized administrators (which would seem to cast the entire model into doubt, but never mind). *Britannica* is edited slowly and by experts, with new articles and edits appearing only occasionally.

The contrast between the two is stark. And while comparing the two encyclopedias raises issues of accuracy, it raises far deeper questions of truth and authority. *Britannica* has built its credibility on several platforms. Through their long history as an organization, they believe they have earned *authority*, authority to declare what is true about 65,000 different topics; they count on the authority of their model in which experts write the articles and teams of dedicated fact-checkers verify them; and they rely on the authority of individual experts to state what is true about any given topic. They maintain that knowledge is authoritative and most accurate when it remains the responsibility of the few, the experts. Wikipedia's

---

*I've had debates of my own. While I was writing this chapter, I was asked to prepare an address on the life of Eric Liddell. Wikipedia's entry on Liddell contained several obvious errors and at least one generalization that could easily have been clarified with a small amount of research ("his parents ... came home on furlough two or three times."). We all know that *Britannica* would have gone to the trouble to find out whether it was two times or three times. It also contained this gem of a (partial) sentence: "in actuality he was suffering from an inoperable brain tumour, to which being overworked and malnourished probably hastened his demise."

founders have taken the opposite view, suggesting that knowledge is most accurate when it is handed over to the masses, when anyone is able to verify accuracy and add to it their own knowledge. They look on the old model with contempt, considering it old-fashioned and outdated. In so doing, they have turned our understanding of knowledge on its head.

Our understandings of truth and authority are changing in this digital world. And as we will see, Wikipedia serves as a microcosm of that kind of change.

Truth, Consensus, Relevance

"God is truth." When we make such a statement, we mean to say that truth is one of the attributes of God. We do not say that God *has* truth, but that God *is* truth, that truth is a part of his very being. The Bible ascribes such truth to each member of the Trinity. Praying to the Father, Jesus said, "And this is eternal life, that they know you the only true God" (John 17:3). Jesus declared himself "the way, and the truth, and the life" (John 14:6) and said the Holy Spirit is "the Spirit of truth" (John 16:13). Clearly truth—a moral truth, a trustworthiness and faithfulness that underlies all that is real and verifiable in the world—is at the very heart of the divine. It is a trait shared equally by Father, Son, and Holy Spirit. And if truth is one of God's attributes, it follows that he is also its source. As God is the starting point for all love and all justice, so, too, he is the source of all truth.

According to Job 37:16, God is perfect in knowledge. To say that God knows all things and that his knowledge is perfect "is to say that he is never mistaken in his perception or understanding of the world: all that he knows and thinks is true and is a correct understanding of the nature of reality. In fact, since God knows all things infinitely well, we can say that the standard of true knowledge is conformity to God's knowledge. If we think the same thing God thinks about anything in the universe, we are thinking truthfully about it."[2]

So what is truth? Truth is what God says. Truth is the moral integrity, the perfection of God expressed in the world. It is that which accords to the actual state of things. It is genuine; it is real; it is pure. It is whatever God thinks. Do you want to know what is true about anything—human sinfulness or the morality of abortion or the existence of the Abominable Snowman? Find out what God thinks about it, and think the same thing. That is truth.

As beings made in the image of God, we are called to imitate him, to be like him. Paul says it most simply of all: "Be imitators of God, as beloved children" (Ephesians 5:1). My son imitates me because I am his father—many of his attributes are my attributes; many of his passions are my passions. And in that way all who are children of the Father are to be like him. Because God is holy, we, too, are to be holy. Because God is love, so we are to be loving, to express love in every way we can. And if God is true, then, of course, we must love the truth, emphasize the truth, and always be seeking truth. All that we say is to be marked by integrity as an expression of the integrity of God.

Truth is an attribute of God that he calls us to imitate so that we can have accurate, reliable knowledge. Though such knowledge can only be partial in the minds and hearts of limited beings like ourselves, we can still be confident that we can know what is true. We can have confidence because this knowledge flows from God as its source. He has given us as our starting point his words, which are always true, always pure (Psalm 12:6). As we hear his words and understand them, we can then begin to think God's thoughts after him so that we can say with the psalmist, "How precious to me are your thoughts, O God! How vast is the sum of them!" (Psalm 139:17). Wayne Grudem tells us how God's truth will guide and inform us as we pursue any kind of knowledge:

> This realization should encourage us in the pursuit of knowledge in all areas of the natural and social sciences and the humanities. Whatever the area of our investigation, when we discover more truth about the nature of reality, we discover more of the truth that God already knows. In this sense we can affirm that "all truth is God's truth" and rejoice whenever the learning or discovery of this truth is used in ways pleasing to God. Growth in knowledge is part of the process of becoming more like God or becoming creatures who are more fully in God's image. Paul tells us that we have put on the "new nature" which, he says, "is being *renewed in knowledge* after the image of its creator" (Colossians 3:10).[3]

God calls us to truth and away from falsehood. He tells us to embrace what is true and to love it as a manifestation of his truth. And he calls us to reject falsehood and to see it as a manifestation of sin and evil. If truth is inherently godlike, error is inherently opposed to him. Truth leads to God, and error leads to Satan, for it is Satan who is the first liar and the father of lies (John 8:44). Grudem offers this warning: "In a society that is exceedingly careless with the truthfulness of spoken words, we as God's children are to imitate our Creator and take great care to be sure that our words are always truthful."[4] Lying is an abomination to God because it mocks his truth. And while factual errors may not carry the same level of moral culpability as outright lies, while they may be unintentional, they are still lies — pointing to a false reality. They still dishonor God.

What does this mean for us as Christians? It means that truth matters. More than any other people, Christians should be clear when they speak and eager to speak the truth. Why? Because we serve the one who *is* truth, and in the Bible we have access to the source of that truth. "The words of the LORD are pure words, like silver refined in a furnace on the ground, purified seven times" (Psalm 12:6). As our words must be true and pure, so must be our knowledge. Truth in all its forms honors God; error in all its forms dishonors him.

And this suggests that we need to be very careful about how we choose the sources of our knowledge, about the way we seek to discern what is true and what is false, about how we determine who has the authority to declare what is true. In the aftermath of the digital explosion, we are seeing radical changes in the conception of truth and what constitutes authority. And so we must pay attention and seek to understand how truth is changing, and how this may be quietly and subtly changing us as well.

We will look at these changes through the lens of two tools that any Internet user is familiar with, tools that pack a powerful one-two punch in seeking out information on the Net. We will look first to the wiki model, as exemplified by Wikipedia, to see how truth in a digital world often comes to us by *consensus*. And then we will turn briefly to search engines, as exemplified by Google, to see how they incline us to associate truth with *relevance*. We will find that Wikipedia is more than a repository of knowledge, and Google is more than a tool to search and find knowledge. Each serves as a "training ground," a means of teaching us what is true and how we can best come to a knowledge of the truth.

▪ Truth by Consensus

Because of its popularity and the way it uses search engine technology to its advantage, Wikipedia is often the first or second result returned by search engines. As I was writing this chapter, I glanced at the pages of the books spread out before me, chose some random words, and performed a Google search for each. *Knowledge, authority,* and *affair* all showed a page from Wikipedia as the very first result; *truth, history,* and *power* all had the entry appear as the second result. Turning to words of theological import, I found that *Jesus, God, justification, Christianity,* and *baptism* also all lead first to Wikipedia. This shows that Wikipedia is now the first to answer many of our most important questions—questions about truth, authority, knowledge, wisdom, power, God, and salvation. As we saw earlier, its 15 million articles draw in 75 million visitors every month.

Wikipedia's success has spawned a long list of imitators, other sites that maintain a similar look and feel and, more importantly, the same wiki format. Because Wikipedia has cornered the market as a general repository of information, most of the imitators are more narrow in scope, catering to just one discipline, whether science or theology. Even dictionaries have become open, with the definitions of words and phrases determined by the crowds (for example, Wiktionary is a lexical extension to Wikipedia, while Urban Dictionary is a repository of slang and hip terms). The wiki model is increasingly regarded as the best means of arriving at truth, of building a repository of knowledge.

The obvious first question is one of accuracy. Do Wikipedia and its many imitators generally get the facts right? Does this new model work? Living in a sinful world, we cannot expect perfection, of course. Our knowledge is incomplete and will always be marked by some error. Yet we want to pursue truth, and the greatest possible truth. Does a wiki get us there?

In many ways it does. Wikipedia is right far more often than it is wrong, truthful far more often than it is marked by error. So before I deal with my concerns, let me be fair and show what the advantages of the wiki model are when compared to a more traditional model. There are certain things that the wiki model does very well.

It is expansive. A traditional encyclopedia has many limitations it must work within, the first of which is a limitation of space. With 65,000 entries, *Encyclopedia Britannica* already comprises thirty-two big and heavy volumes.* And because each article must be prepared, edited, and fact-checked by a staff member, the number of articles must be relatively few. There are issues related both to physical space and to editorial bandwidth. Not so with Wikipedia. Because it uses electronic storage rather than paper, there is near-infinite room for expansion; because entries can be created by anyone and immediately published, there is no need for editorial intervention or approval. The wiki model has proven that it can be much bigger, much more expansive in its scope.

It relies on more sources. The wiki model does not depend on the knowledge, the time, or the goodwill of a few experts. Instead, it allows anyone with knowledge to add, change, clarify, edit. I recently observed that in the

---

*If the *Britannica* had as many entries as Wikipedia, it would fill something like 10,000 volumes and cost nearly a half million dollars for a single set. There would have to be more than 300 volumes just to cover *A*.

Wikipedia entry for Eric Liddell, it was stated that he ran the 400 meter final in the 1924 Olympics clutching a piece of paper on which someone had written a few inspirational words. This is how the event was shown in the movie *Chariots of Fire*, but I knew this wasn't historically accurate (though even in the movie half the shots of the final race show him clutching the paper; the other half do not—watch for it next time). Because this article is built on the wiki model, I could immediately edit the entry to correct this mistake. I am no expert on Eric Liddell but had recently read a couple of his biographies and had learned that though he appreciated the note, he did not run with it. Inherent in a wiki is the understanding that we all have knowledge and that each of us can contribute to that knowledge. This accords with what Protestants have long believed about the priesthood of all believers, that God dispenses truth not to just a select few but to all of his people.

It is cheap. Because the wiki model depends on the labor of the masses and does not pay contributors, editors, or administrators, it has very low overhead. This allows the Internet to have more wikis, more repositories of knowledge dedicated to more subjects. And it allows us to access it for free.

It is responsive. The wiki model is fluid, able to respond quickly. Entries can be changed swiftly in response to new realities. When a celebrity dies, his Wikipedia entry is often changed within moments.* That same entry in a traditional encyclopedia may not be changed for several years. When I noted the inaccuracy about Eric Liddell, I did not need to notify an editorial panel; I could simply make the change myself, a process that took less than one minute.

It is convenient. Wikipedia is available in its entirety from any device that has Internet access. I do not need to carry thirty-two hardbound volumes with me; I can simply carry my iPhone. The site's format also offers the convenience of interlinking—one page often linking to hundreds of others. As I research one topic, I can quickly find information about related topics.

The wiki model does have much to commend it. Whether looking for general information on Wikipedia or searching for information about a particular scientific fact through a wiki dedicated to a narrow discipline, this model is able to create and share vast amounts of information—and this information tends to be factual.

And yet it is not without its drawbacks, some of which are quite serious.

---

*This ability does not come without drawbacks. On many occasions, false reports of celebrity deaths have appeared in the news, and the associated Wikipedia articles have been immediately updated with this false information.

It ignores human nature. The wiki model inherently assumes that humans are generally good and that they will work together to achieve the greatest good for the greatest number. This ignores what the Bible tells us, that as sinful humans we are predominantly selfish, looking out for our own good ahead of the good of others. While our individual actions may assist others, we are still inherently and essentially sinful. We are not good people who occasionally do bad things, but bad people who sometimes do good things. The wiki model has had to account for human nature and respond to it in different ways, even ways that seem to cast the whole model in doubt. As just one example, certain pages have become so controversial or have seen so much vandalism that they have been locked so only administrators can edit them.

It offers too little review. The sheer volume of information that tends to accumulate makes it impossible to patrol it all, to ensure quality and accuracy. As of the day I turned in the manuscript for this book, Wikipedia had just 1,742 administrators tasked with overseeing more than three million English articles; tens of thousands or hundreds of thousands of articles may be changed on any given day. Though there are no set qualifications to take on this position, administrators have the final say over articles, determining if they must be locked down, changed, or deleted. When we have a model that ignores human nature and combine it with too little oversight, we will inevitably run into problems related to the misuse of authority. Wikipedia admits the failings in its model: "Older articles tend to grow more comprehensive and balanced; newer articles may contain misinformation, unencyclopedic [sic] content, or vandalism. Awareness of this aids obtaining valid information and avoiding recently added misinformation."[5] And yet this warning is buried deep within the Wikipedia system. Very few people who read its articles are aware that newer articles frequently contain significant misinformation.

It is too subjective. In 2007, Virgil Griffith released a tool he called WikiScanner. The purpose was to link Wikipedia edits with the computer addresses of the people or organizations that had made changes to articles. The results were stunning, showing that many corporations and politicians—those with a vested interest in a certain topic—were constantly monitoring and changing certain articles within Wikipedia. Computers from inside the headquarters of the Church of Scientology had removed critiques of the church from the article on Scientology; computers from inside the Vatican allegedly changed an article on Sinn Féin president Gerry Adams. The anonymity of Wikipedia and the way in which it allows anyone to edit articles entail that people will seek to protect their own interests in the world's most important repository of information. Some believe that as wikis mature, objectivity will increase. I find this difficult to believe. As wikis mature, their importance will increase, and so it will become more critical that they contain not necessarily what *is* true about us but what we want others to *believe is* the truth.

It ignores authority. While Christians believe in the priesthood of all believers, we also believe in honoring God-given authority, a topic I will discuss shortly. The wiki model levels authority structures, assigning no value to age, experience, or education. When editing an entry on justification that explains how God saves his people, the ten-year-old child stands on equal footing with the most eminent theologian. In this way, it offers a kind of radical egalitarianism seemingly at odds with biblical authority structures—and with just plain common sense.

It redefines truth. The most dangerous problem is that the wiki model gives us a whole new understanding of truth. What is truth? Truth in this model is nearly indistinguishable from consensus. Because there are no experts and because "facts" do not have to be proven, the model brings with it a level of uncertainty about what is true. When truth is in dispute, when a piece of information is turned one way and then another, the deciding factor is not whether the fact can be proven from an authoritative source; it is what the majority agrees on or an administrator decides on, even if that administrator has no knowledge about the topic. *The wiki model tells us that truth is what the majority determines it to be.* If 75 percent of us determine that Eric Liddell ran with a piece of paper in his hand, the model offers no way of contesting it. In this way it democratizes truth, subtly teaching us that truth can be found through the majority opinion. By requesting footnotes, it tells us that what has been put in print is true and, conversely, that what has not been printed has not been proven. *It tells us that all sources are equal in authority.* If someone can find a quote saying that Liddell ran with a piece of paper in his hand, he has every right to contest and overrule my edit.

Even some in Hollywood recognize that this is problematic. Stephen Colbert coined the word *wikiality*, stating, "Together we can create a reality that we all agree on—the reality we just agreed on."[6] Colbert understands what far too many miss: when we look at the way the Internet defines truth, consensus reigns. Truth does not have its source in God; it has its source in *us*—the majority opinion.

The younger you are, the less likely you are to understand this. Younger generations have little sense of the distinction between old sources of knowledge and today's newer sources. They have even less of a sense that Wikipedia is more likely to be radically wrong than *Britannica*. Admittedly, I frequently access Wikipedia, but I always regard it as a nonauthoritative source of information. Its convenience appeals to me more than its authority. It is handy, but I rarely allow it to be the final word. Instead, it is a starting point for knowledge, not a destination. Wikis, we find, are better at communicating information than knowledge. The more they attempt to speak to what is true, the more troublesome they become.

Academic institutions have had to wrestle with the reality of a wiki world. Oliver Kamm warns of the danger inherent in allowing consensus to serve as the arbiter of truth: "Intellectual inquiry involves testing ideas against the canons of evidence," but "Wikipedia recognizes no intrinsic value in competence or knowledge; its guiding principle is agreement rather than truth.... Wikipedia has no means of arbitrating between different claims, other than how many people side with one position rather than another. That ethos is fatal to the advancement of learning."[7]

Some schools regard any use of Wikipedia as an automatic fail; others consider it equal to any other encyclopedia. In an interview with *Business Week*, Wikipedia's founder Jimmy Wales cautions students against quoting Wikipedia: "No, I don't think people should cite it, and I don't think people should cite Britannica either—the error rate there isn't very good. People shouldn't be citing encyclopedias in the first place."[8] He may be right, but the reason that many teachers in days past told students to avoid encyclopedias had nothing to do with accuracy—it was to discourage laziness! Teachers wanted their students to go directly to the sources, not rely on summaries of those sources. Wales misses the point.

Consensus opinion and Scripture are often opposed to one another. The consensus today holds that the world we see was shaped by an impersonal process of evolution through which all that exists has come to be. But the Bible tells us that it was lovingly fashioned by a good Creator. The consensus tells us that humans are essentially good, that the Bible is a human construct, and that human life begins sometime after the moment of conception. In all these things, the consensus is directly opposed to God's truth.

▪ Truth by Relevance

If consensus is the chief arbiter of truth on the Internet today, relevance follows close behind. When we type a search into Google or any other major search engine, we are asking it to look through the trillions of pages on the

Internet to determine which of them is most relevant to that word or term. Google's brilliant innovation in search, the one that has allowed them to become far and away the most popular search engine, is in finding a way to measure relevance. Those who have attempted to study Google's formula for ascertaining relevance will not be surprised to know that it is a product of brilliant mathematical minds. It is a mathematical formula that determines what I will find when I search for *truth* on the Internet. If I type "What is truth?" into Google, Google will feed me the most *relevant* results. Ironically enough, the second result will be the Wikipedia article for *truth* (an article in which *truth* answers to the *consensus* of Wikipedia's readers), which will offer a Christian conception of truth as *just one option* among many.

This is one more way in which truth becomes *egalitarian* on the Internet. The magic formula Google has created (and constantly refines) places a strong emphasis on links from one page to another. Every time I link to one page from my own website, Google registers that as a vote. If I create a link from my site using the words "world's greatest Maple Leafs fan" and link to my friend Julian's blog, Google registers this as a vote through which I am stating, "Julian is the world's greatest fan of the Toronto Maple Leafs." If I asked my 5,000 Facebook friends to do the same thing, we would register 5,000 votes for Julian. Later on, when someone performs a search for "Maple Leafs fan," they may very well find that Google now considers him as such. This would not be true (as it happens, Julian despises the Maple Leafs), but it would be relevant. Google makes no distinction.[9]

Interestingly, Google's trust and authority algorithms work by assigning trust to a domain and a page within that domain based on the sites linking to each one. For this to work, Google has to somehow determine the sites that have the highest authority and that offer the greatest level of trust. These are the sites that have the most impact in determining what is true according to their formula. Not surprisingly, a site like Wikipedia ranks very high in Google's algorithm, one of just a handful of sites that achieve a PageRank of 9 (10 is the highest possible PageRank, but fewer than fifteen sites in the entire world qualify).

▪ Truth's Shaking Foundation

Wikis measure truth by consensus, while search engines measure truth by relevance. Both of them highlight issues related to discovering what is true in a digital world. The issue before us is not whether Wikipedia is good or evil or whether search engines are good or evil. The issue is one of truth, of the way our technologies are changing our very conception of truth. This happened with the advent of the photograph as well. In an age of print, we believed what we read. But in an age of photography, an age of images, somewhere along the way we decided that a picture was worth 1,000 words—that images carried more weight and authority in the arena of truth. We began to believe what we *saw* instead of what we *read*, often demanding visual evidence before we would believe anything at all. Somewhere along the way the image changed the way we understand truth.

Having seen the success of the wiki model, some people are now asking, "Can we understand all of human knowledge as a wiki?" Might digital technology hold the key to help us understand who we are? As Christians, we know that this avenue is nothing more than a dead end. Knowledge and truth cannot be democratized; they flow from the God who is truth. As we create and use digital technologies like wikis and search engines to access information, we must guard against the danger of allowing them to re-create us in their own image. If we fail, these changed conceptions of truth will change us, re-forming our very understanding of what truth is and how we can know it.

The answer to this challenge is not to simply reject wikis and search engines. I would never claim that the old models were always right—even *Encyclopedia Britannica* contains errors. We have never been able to trust *everything* we read or *everything* we hear, which is why the Bible continually tells us to exercise discernment, to learn to distinguish between good and evil, truth and error. Yet these new technologies are heralding an important shift. While we've never been able to trust everything presented as fact, we've been able to trust *the system* through which we have come to know facts. Today that entire system is being thrown into doubt.

As the foundation of truth is changing, we need to be very careful that we do not allow it to change us as well. As Christians we know what is true because we know *who* is true. We know the source of truth, and we have access to him through the words he has given us. We know that consensus and relevance may imitate truth and at times properly reflect what is true. But all truth ultimately flows from the one who is Truth.

Authority

Closely related to truth is the issue of authority. The Bible tells us that "there is no authority except from God, and those that exist have been instituted by God" (Romans 13:1). Just as truth flows out of the character of God, so too does authority. All authority is delegated by God. If we wish to honor God, we must first learn to honor those who have been placed in authority over us. There are clear spiritual consequences when we refuse to do this: "Whoever resists the authorities resists what God has appointed, and those who resist will incur judgment" (13:2).

God is the ultimate authority in the universe. His power stems from his act of creation, and "it is in his revelation that God's authority is to be found: revelation is, therefore, the key to ultimate authority."[10] In his creation God shows himself as both moral and redemptive, and through the creation God calls everyone to obedience. For created beings, authority is never assumed. It is power given in trust by God, given as a responsibility before him.

If all authority originates with God, then all authority must be subject first and foremost to God. My children are called by God to submit to my authority, but if I require of them something that contradicts a higher authority, they may and must submit to that higher authority. This places the weight of responsibility on those who hold authority to lead well. It places responsibility on all who follow them to constantly remind them that they are answerable to God. Submission to authority—even to sinful, corrupt human leadership—is possible because we understand that all submission is ultimately a way of submitting to God, through his delegates.

As sinful human beings, we tend to fight against authority, to regard it as an inherently evil thing. But as Christians, we see authority in a different light. While we recognize the detrimental impact of sin and the evil that resides in the hearts of men and women, we also see authority as a gracious gift of God. Authority is a gift through which God orders relationships in a way that brings glory to him. Authority is about *order*, maintaining proper structures of relationship so it is clear who is leading, taking responsibility, and being accountable for the choices that are made. It is about *protection*, caring for those with less knowledge, wisdom, or strength. And ultimately, it is about the *character* of God, showing the world that God is a God of order rather than chaos.

If God is the ultimate authority and the one from whom all authority stems, then anything that threatens to disrupt existing authority structures, whether for good or for ill, merits our attention as Christians. Great shifts in authority structures merit serious thought and reflection. Why? Because authority is closely related to truth.

▪ Radical Egalitarianism

When we think of authority, we naturally think of hierarchy, of differing levels of authority arranged in a vertical structure. In days of old, kings or despots maintained power and demanded our submission, and under them were many different levels of sacred and secular government. Today we have democratic governments that, though elected by the masses, continue to wield this same kind of top-down authority.

We have long understood that authority is related to knowledge in the same way. Knowledge has typically come from above, from the chosen few, the experts. Professors, in positions of authority, told us what was *true* about history or chemistry. Pastors, chosen authorities in the church, told us what was true about the Bible. Psychiatrists, accredited authorities on the human psyche, told us what was true about the mind. But all of this is now shifting in the digital world. As we have seen, it is now the consensus of the masses that informs our understanding. In the place of *few* experts we have *many* amateurs—leaving us with what one author has termed "the cult of the amateur."[11]

In my bookcase I have several volumes labeled *systematic theology*. Each of these has been written by a venerable theologian, a man who has spent a lifetime studying the Bible. Their knowledge of theology and their systematization of it are distilled into a magnum opus of a few hundred pages. But this is an old model that is quickly becoming outdated. As we have seen, today it is the crowd that creates knowledge, that determines what is right and wrong. The systematic theologies of the future will be crowdsourced, with any one of us contributing, any one of us changing the words of the greatest theologian.* In the end it is not truth that will prevail, but consensus.

In 1994, Wayne Grudem published his *Systematic Theology*, a volume that has become a go-to resource for many Christians. His decades of study, his thirty years as a seminary professor, his postgraduate degrees, were distilled into this book. It is regarded as an excellent systematic theology— authoritative on many of its subjects. Grudem earned the right to write this volume through his long years of experience, his diligent study, and the respect of peers who affirmed his skill as a theologian.

In 2007, a Wikipedia contributor operating under the pseudonym Essjay was found to have made false claims about his academic credentials and professional experience on his Wikipedia user page and to a journalist

---

*The term *crowdsourcing* refers to crowd-outsourcing—asking a crowd, usually via the Internet, to collaborate on a task that formerly would have been completed by a single organization or individual.

from *The New Yorker*. He was found to have edited some 16,000 articles and to have used his false credentials and experience as leverage to solve disputes about Wikipedia content related to theology (though, as we know, this ought to have no bearing within the Wikipedia model). Essjay, later identified as Ryan Jordan, claimed to hold doctoral degrees in theology and canon law and said that he worked as a tenured professor at a private university. When Jordan eventually came clean, it was found that he was a twenty-four-year-old college dropout with no academic credentials and, obviously, no teaching experience. He had no authority in any traditional sense.

Reacting to the inevitable fallout, Wikipedia cofounder Jimmy Wales responded, "Mr. Ryan [*sic*] was a friend, and still is a friend. He is a young man, and he has offered me a heartfelt personal apology, which I have accepted. I hope the world will let him go in peace to build an honorable life and reputation."[12] Wales denied that the situation exposed any inherent weakness in Wikipedia's model. In fact, if there was any weakness exposed, it was in the people who continued to believe that the academic credentials actually meant anything in the Wikipedia model.

Though we cannot prove it, it is entirely likely that more people viewed information posted on Wikipedia by Ryan Jordan than have read Grudem's *Systematic Theology*. This is the result of the redefinition of authority that is happening through digital technology today. Even when Jordan was found to have fraudulent credentials, Wales was unconcerned. Jordan's false claims to authority did nothing, in Wales's mind, to negate his contributions.

Book reviews are another area where we see traditional authority structures undermined. It is not unusual today to read of authors whose books have been pilloried on Amazon, very nearly a death sentence when it comes to sales. In April 2010, historian Orlando Figes admitted to having posted negative reviews of books written by his rivals. While he offered wholehearted apologies, the fact is that he could do it and that it could make a great difference in sales and in perceived authority. It is not unremarkable that Figes apologized only after being found out.

New digital technologies function as a great leveler, reducing the authority of the expert and elevating the authority of the amateur. The lifelong theologian has no more authority than the young child; the teacher has no more authority than the pupil; the parent has no more authority than the child. As we undermine the authority inherent in knowledge, how long will it be before we undermine authority in other areas of life?

The old authority structures, those top-down structures where experts led amateurs, has now faded into the twilight. In its place we have *crowdsourcing*, the cult of the amateur. Book and movie reviews, once the domain of the professional reviewer, are now the realm of the unknown blogger or the random buyer. The professor in his lecture hall sits before an audience of fact-checkers who, at a moment's notice and a few taps of their fingers, can validate or invalidate his facts. Citizen journalists interpret the news more quickly (and sometimes with better skill) than the highly paid journalists at major news outlets.

Truth in an Old Way

In 2005, three young filmmakers from small-town New York pooled $2,000 they had saved up and created an eighty-minute movie called *Loose Change*. In this movie, first conceived as fiction but released in the form of documentary, the men claimed that the 9/11 attacks were organized and carried out by the Bush administration. In their version of events, pieced together from actual footage, out-of-context quotes, and since-discredited news clips, they claimed that at least one of the American Airlines Flight 11 hijackers was found alive after the crash and that United Airlines Flight 95 did not crash in a Pennsylvania field but was instead redirected to Cleveland. And, of course, the Twin Towers did not collapse because of the impact of the aircraft, but because of explosives that had been planted in advance. The film is still available on YouTube, having been watched over 4 million times there and tens of millions of times on other sites. It has been watched and believed—one of the first and most influential conspiracy theory takes on 9/11.

Not surprisingly, all of these claims have been disproved by the final report of the 9/11 Commission. This report cost $15 million to create, took two years to compile, and was written by two governors, four congressmen, three former White House officials, and two special counsels.[13] The report found no evidence of government conspiracy or complicity.

It seems obvious which of these—the film or the report—is more credible. But why? In a traditional *Britannica* world, we would cede to the experts, to those who have credibility that comes with age, experience, and position. The commission's report offers facts to back its claims; it offers evidence. But in the wiki world, a world where truth and authority have been transformed, many will cede instead to consensus. Facts are nearly meaningless since my source is equal to your source. You point to the 9/11 report and declare it the truth, while I point to the film and declare it the truth. And then we allow consensus to determine which is right.

This is not a huge concern if we continue to understand truth in an old way—if we understand that truth and authority flow from God to humans. There is nothing to fear from Wikipedia if I continue to demand that what is stated there as fact is proven in an adequate way—if it refers to authoritative sources. But there is everything to fear from Wikipedia when it demands that we change our very understanding of truth, insisting that truth comes by consensus, that every person holds equal authority, and that every source is equal to every other. Search engines give no cause for concern as long as we understand that they offer a mathematical means of linking relevance to truth. But search engines cause concern when our very understanding of truth sees the consensus of relevance as the means of determining what is true.

APPLICATION
Truth and Authority

In this chapter, we have looked at issues related to truth and authority and have seen how the Internet upends traditional understandings of both.

Theology tells us that all truth is God's truth—that God is the source of all truth and that all that is true is somehow a reflection of him. It also tells us that Satan is the enemy of truth and that he does not just seek to replace individual truths with lies, but, even more, he seeks to undermine our entire conception of truth. If he can undermine truth, if he can undermine authority, he can undermine the church.

Our *theory* of technology tells us that the medium is the message, that using a wiki and a search engine will eventually shape us. The ideas inherent in a search engine—that truth is known by relevance—or the ideas inherent in a wiki—that truth is known by consensus—will quietly work their ways into our hearts and minds.

Yet our *experience* of technology shows that we are increasingly reliant on search engines and wikis, that these new technologies constantly stand between us and what we seek to know. They mediate truth to us.

We see, then, that we need to be exceedingly careful that we know and understand and defend not just what is true but the very idea of truth, the very understanding that all truth flows out of the character of God. Truth is not what is relevant or what is popular, but *what God thinks*.

Know the One who is truth. Before we can be equipped to know what is true, we must know *who* is true. And in order to know him, we must find him in his Word, the Bible. The first commitment of one who seeks to know what is true is commitment to the Bible.

Be aware. When seeking to know what is true, be aware that Wikipedia and search engines, and the technologies that will eventually supersede them, have ideas embedded within them. Know that when you search for important terms on Google, it speaks with no real authority on what is true and what is false. Know when you access Wikipedia or any other source of knowledge that it is crowdsourced and subject to all of the failings of that model. The more important the subject matter, the less you should rely on Wikipedia and other similar sites.

Celebrate authority. Truth is very closely related to authority, since those with the most authority in a given area are the ones most likely to know what is true. Christians must understand this relationship and be willing to do the hard work of learning what is true from the best sources. While Wikipedia and its peers offer great convenience, they are simply too problematic to be able to trust them in the way we can trust traditional sources.

QUESTIONS FOR REFLECTION

1. Which model of encyclopedia do you find more compelling? Why? Which do you rely on more often?

2. Why is it tempting to accept the consensus as truth? How would you defend the biblical understanding of truth against the consensus opinion?

3. In what ways might our use of Wikipedia or the search engines, over time, shape our very understanding of how we can know what is true? Can you think of any examples?

4. How has the radical egalitarianism of the web, the great leveling of authority, influenced the way you think of pastors or professors or other spiritual authorities in your life?

CHAPTER 9

SEEING and BEING SEEN (Visibility and Privacy)

I live not too far from Toronto Pearson International Airport. Most mornings, and especially very cold mornings, I can look into the sky above my home and see the contrails, the vapor trails the jets leave behind them as they slice through the air. It is rarely difficult to tell where the planes have come from or the direction they are going; I can just follow the trails.

In the same way, we leave data trails behind us in this digital world, long trails of purchases, searches, photographs, clicks, and so much more. The data collection points are too numerous to count. Yet wherever we go and whatever we do, they follow behind us like contrails follow airplanes. They tell where we have been and often tell where we are going.

In this chapter, I want to look at issues related to visibility and privacy—the things we do online, the trails we leave behind us, and the strange reality that we crave both privacy and visibility in this new digital reality. In the aftermath of the digital explosion, we love to see one another and be seen, and we are constantly tracked and monitored—by friend, by foe, and by those with a vested interest in knowing as much about us as they possibly can.

I am writing today from a café just a few minutes from my home. Though the staff here can be decidedly unpleasant, the food is good, the Internet is rock-solid, and the change of location allows me to write in a different context than my home office. It is still early in the day, and so far I have accomplished little more than running through my usual morning routine. After spending some time reading the Bible and praying, after eating a quick breakfast and saying good-bye to my wife and children, I walked down the hill to this café so I could work on my book.

Before I began, though, I spent a few minutes reading the headlines at a news site. I browsed through the latest blog articles collected by my RSS reader and checked in at Facebook to see what my friends have been up to. Even in these few, innocuous activities, I have left behind a trail of data. My cell phone carrier has tracked me as I've walked from home to the café, and even now it can get a read on my location to within a few meters—certainly an accurate enough read to know that I am in this building. A few minutes ago, my iPhone sent Apple twelve hours' worth of location information based on GPS, WiFi connections, and cell phone towers. Facebook knows the Internet address I have visited from, knows what computer I am using, knows each of the ads they showed to me, and knows that I did not click on any of them. Google knows what blogs I looked at this morning and knows that I did a search or two along the way. MasterCard knows where I am—or at least they knew where I was about fifteen minutes ago, since they now have a record of the purchase I made (quite a good fried egg sandwich, if you must know). A security camera at the bank next door has stored some footage of me as I deposited a check into their instant teller. All of this data has been recorded somewhere—in many somewheres, actually. And this data is likely to remain there forever. It will be the exception rather than the rule if the data is ever deleted.

While all of this information was collected in the background as I was going about other business, I've also been deliberate in making public certain information about myself. I left a comment at a friend's blog, written under my name and stamped with a date and time and Internet address. I commented on a friend's Facebook status and dashed off a Twitter update that I thought was hilarious (but which seems to have fallen flat—again). I published a post on my own blog and wrote a short batch of e-mails, responding to the messages that came in overnight. In each of these things, I have left behind records of what I was doing, when I was doing it, where I was doing it from—and I've done so knowingly.

That this data trail exists does not concern me too much. After all, it is mere data that exists in its parts in a hundred different places. Somewhere in a database, MasterCard has recorded that at 9:02 a.m. I spent a few dollars at this café. In another database, Google has a record of my search; and in still another database, my cell phone carrier has a record of where I was at this time and where I was a half hour ago. These are disparate little pieces of data, all of which mean very little in isolation.

Yet together they point to a larger reality: *we are under constant surveillance.* Our lives are lived before the public today in a way they never have been before.

Wherever you go and whatever you do, you leave a trail of physical evidence behind—fingerprints, dead skin cells, hairs that have fallen out. This is the kind of evidence that investigators hope to find when attempting to solve a crime. A fingerprint or a hair from my head links me to a specific location. We know that such evidence exists, but it does not concern us (provided we have not recently committed a crime) because there is no one who routinely tracks all of that information, who follows behind us to collect the hairs and skin cells in order to build a profile of us, to figure out where we have been and what we have done there. And yet in our digital lives, there are many ways in which we are tracked and profiled, in which people attempt to figure out what we've done, where we've been, and who we are based on the data trails we leave behind us.

This calls us to react in two different ways. First, we need simply to be aware of this fact and react accordingly, working to ensure that we keep important information safe. We do this for the sake of protecting ourselves and our families. Second, we need to understand that our lives are public in an unprecedented way and that through such visibility we may bring honor to God, or we may bring reproach to his name.

The Numerati

Think of the data you leave behind you every day, the data that falls from you like skin cells from your body or leave behind like fingerprints when you "touch" a website or a cell phone. I just mentioned a few of the ways in which I leave data behind me in my day-to-day life through using my computer, accessing websites, and carrying a mobile phone. We all leave behind endless little bits of data, small pieces of it in a million different places.

As we transitioned to a digital, computer-driven world, we saw that computers were quickly growing in power and ability, and we made the conscious decision to add them to our homes and offices. We did so under one defining condition: "We had to render everything we sent, the very stuff of our lives, into ones and zeros. That's how we came to deliver our riches, the key to communications on earth, to the masters of the symbolic language."[1] To put our lives into computers, we had to reduce our lives to data, to those zeroes and ones that make sense to computers. Our words and pictures, sounds and images, are all reduced to bits and bytes and stored on digital media.

Gone are the days when our photographs were found in albums on the coffee table, when our thoughts were recorded in diaries stashed in a bedside table; gone are the days when our correspondence was sent in sealed envelopes and our videos resided only on tapes. Today everything is increasingly migrating online. As all of these forms of media move online, they are digitized. And digital data is relatively easy to mine—certainly far easier than combing through physical photos and ink-on-paper letters. Computers can programmatically comb through all of the data and mine from it important and telling bits of information.

In all of this digitization there has been a cost. "Now these mathematicians and computer scientists are in a position to rule the information of our lives."[2] Author Stephen Baker uses the phrase *the Numerati* to describe this whole new class of people—mathematicians and computer scientists who are hired by companies to collect and to mine through all of this personal data. Their task is to combine the small pieces to form some kind of a cohesive whole, to form from it profiles of individuals and entire elements of society. And this information is then used to sell products to us, to grant us (or refuse to grant us) credit cards, to send us spam e-mails, or, in worst cases, to humiliate us or even to steal our identities. These are people who sift through all of these bits and build their own version of *us*, their own understanding of who we are.

As you know, data is just data, words and numbers that mean very little on their own. Yet when it is collated and collected, sorted through and analyzed, it can be very revealing. It can show patterns of behavior, likes and dislikes. It can even be predictive, allowing people to prognosticate about future behavior (and, indeed, as this chapter was in the editing process, a major news outlet ran a story about new software that can analyze various types of data to predict when crimes will be committed and who will commit them). The more data these Numerati have available to them, the more accurate their profiles can be. And so they seek to gather it from as many points as possible.

Consider all of the data people add to their Facebook profiles, and you will quickly see why Facebook is such a valuable company—it has massive amounts of the most personal information on each one of us. It knows our hobbies and religions, our friend and family connections, our photographs and videos, and details of our activities as we've updated our statuses. It knows our high schools and colleges, our birth dates and anniversaries. Facebook has value simply in its expansive user base, but more so, in the information it contains. This information is a gold mine to advertisers, to those who want to present their products to us.

Google is a company built almost entirely on mathematics. The answer Google provides to you, the list of sites they deem most relevant to your search, are chosen largely through mathematical formulas. The brilliance of Google is their ability to capture data about us and to find ways of turning that data into money—lots of money. Google and similar companies continually draw to themselves the best minds in math and science and assign these people to find new and creative ways of interacting with the data.

The job of the Numerati is to build mathematical models of all of us, to reduce us to numbers, statistics, and profiles. Retailers maintain records of every dollar we spend at their stores; cell phone companies record the calls we make and the locations we make them from; doctors maintain extensive logs of our visits—what we discussed with them, how they treated us, Facebook maintains a record of our past relationships, the messages we've sent to old boyfriends or girlfriends, the things we said before we were Christians and things we have said since.

Consider, as an example, the customer loyalty card you got from your local grocery store. What is its purpose? Obviously the company wants to make you a loyal customer so you continue to spend your money at their store. The card grants you a discount, meaning that you are likely to continue shopping there. But what's the trade-off? In this case, the trade-off is privacy; you are granting to the store extensive information about you and about your shopping habits. The job of the Numerati somewhere in a corporate office is to look through all of this data and to build a profile for each of us that will tell them who we are, what we want, and how they can get us to buy more of it.

The Numerati have nothing but data, nothing but numbers available to them. And from these numbers they build a profile of each one of us. In a strange but very real way, they reduce us to numbers; they reduce us to data. Do you see how this works? These people have never met us; they may not even know our names, and yet through the data trails we leave behind us, they can build strangely accurate profiles, predictive profiles, even. They may know what we will do and what we will buy (or, at least, what we are most likely to buy) before we do.

A couple of years ago, my wife and I went to our bank to apply for a small line of credit. We were hoping to do some work on the house and, for the first time, were looking at using a small amount of credit to push this work from the distant future into the immediate future. We sat with a personal banker and watched as he filled out form after form on his computer. He asked for numbers, which we gave to him, and he punched them into his computer. With a flourish, he hit the submit button and a few seconds later said, "I'm sorry, but we are not able to give you a loan at this time." I pressed him to see if there was anything he could do, any factor we needed to change. I reminded him that we had been banking at this location for many years without ever bouncing a check or overdrawing our accounts. But all he could tell us was that the computer had rejected our application. He inputted the numbers and found that the numbers somehow didn't add up.

We have all experienced this, I think, and it may seem quite unremarkable. Yet there is something that *ought* to be remarkable. In applying for a loan, the bank had reduced us to numbers. We were not people who had paid every bill and met every obligation. Instead, we were a series of numbers — incomes and expenses and liabilities. In the end, a computer processed the numbers and found that for one reason or another we simply did not qualify as borrowers. And that was that. The bankers had no ability to change the rules and no right to plead our case. The numbers had spoken. It was strangely distressing and dehumanizing.

Facebook, Google, grocery stores, and banks are in the business of quantifying us.[3] They are offering up a mathematical model of humanity, a model that can tell them what we do, who we love, how we behave, and, in some sense, who we really are.

How might it affect us and our society if we believe, as do these Numerati, that we can best understand people, not by meeting with them, not by knowing them in any real sense, but simply by studying their data? Am I simply my data?

In a not-so-subtle way, the Numerati are teaching us to see other people, not as real flesh-and-blood people created in the image of God, but as objects—numerical data that can be used to satisfy our own purposes. Perhaps you work in an environment where it is common to talk about "consumers" or a "target audience" and refer to large groups of people as nothing more than numbers or statistics on a page. As useful as this information may be at times, we should be careful to guard against the subtle influence this practice can have on our attitude toward others.

The Bible assures us that people are not simply objects we use for our own selfish purposes. Each of us has been created in God's image and for his purposes. Each of us is an individual lovingly crafted by the hand of a Creator. David sang of the wonder of this:

> For you formed my inward parts;
>   you knitted me together in my mother's womb.
> I praise you, for I am fearfully and wonderfully made.

Psalm 139:13 – 14

Time may well show that one of the digital world's greatest effects on human beings has been to depersonalize us, to tear away our humanity in favor of 1's and 0's—to make us little more than their data. And increasingly we relate to one another as if we are not real people, not people with thoughts and feelings and emotions but people who are barely people at all. We relate to one another as if we are all computers, as if we are merely digital.

In the Public Eye

In June 2010, Congressman Bob Etheridge was walking down a sidewalk in Washington, D.C. when he was approached by two young men, both of whom had video cameras in hand. One man asked Etheridge, "Do you fully support the Obama agenda?" He answered, "Who are you?" and quickly grabbed at one of the men. He grabbed him by the wrist, the arm, and then the back of the neck, all the while asking, "Who are you?" Eventually he released the young man and went on his way. While there was no damage done to the people or to their equipment, Etheridge quickly became a YouTube sensation. The video was seen millions of times and quickly appeared all over the media. The situation would have been unremarkable and would have gone largely unnoticed, except for the fact that millions of people were watching. With the public visibility of his apparently unprovoked assault, he was forced to issue a contrite apology.

As a politician, Etheridge learned a harsh lesson—he needs to be on his best behavior when in public. His life is more public than ever. Even the slightest misstep can change his life. And so it is for any of us. We do not need to be politicians to be intimidated by, to be concerned about, the growth in visibility brought about by this digital age.

Digital Detritus

How many people in the world know your gender, your zip code, and your birth date? Think back to all of the forms you've filled out online, the accounts you have created and long-since forgotten about. Just these three pieces of information are enough to uniquely identify 87 percent of the United States population—which is to say that these three pieces of information, when taken together, can usually lead to a name, an address, a telephone number. They lead to a real person. They lead to you.

But there isn't a lot you can do about it. Giving away these little bits of information, leaving a digital trail, is a part of life in this world. As long as we are going to live with and through our digital technologies, they will continue to leave evidence of our interaction with them.

We do well simply to be aware that we do leave trails behind—trails that tell about who we are. Many a husband or wife has been proven a liar by his or her data trail. Where they insisted they were one thing, the data they left behind them showed them to be another. What is fascinating about all of this data is that in many ways we are our data. We cannot neatly separate ourselves from our data as if we are one thing but our data proves we are another. I may be a fine Christian gentleman, a family man and pastor, but if my data shows that I routinely visit pornographic websites, my data, not my presentation of myself, will show who I really am. In Matthew 7:16, Jesus said, "You will recognize them by their fruits." Perhaps today we might add, "You will recognize them by their data." Consider that this trail follows you and speaks to who you really are in those moments when no one can see you.

And be aware that the data you leave behind may be used against you or in ways you would not expect. Be cautious with what you reveal about yourself. You will tend to trust your grocery store and not mind that they maintain a complete list of everything you've bought using your loyalty card.

But let's imagine for a moment that somewhere within the IT department of that company is a disgruntled employee, one who is nearly ready to resign but who wants to go out with a bang. He may have access to the records of millions of customers, and he may see fit to make them public, to copy them to a website. Or he may be a neighbor who is angry with you and who looks up your records and makes public certain information about you. Such things have happened, and they are happening today.

Consider: In 2006, America Online made an epic misjudgment. As part of a research project headed by Dr. Abdur Chowdhury, the company made available to the public a massive amount of data culled from their search engine—the search history of 650,000 users over a three-month period. This totaled some 21 million searches. Before releasing the data, they anonymized it, stripping away user names and replacing names with numbers, so that a user with a name like timc2000 simply became User #75636534. Yet because of the often-personal nature of the data, it did not take long before many of those abstract numbers were linked to real names, an obvious and serious violation of privacy and confidentiality. Within days, AOL realized its mistake and withdrew the data, but already it had been copied and uploaded elsewhere on the Internet, where today it lives on in infamy.

Some of the search histories were dark and disturbing, others unremarkable in every way. Still others were strangely amusing. It was often possible to reconstruct a person's life, at least in part, from what they searched for over a period of time. Consider this user:

- shipping pets 2006-03-01 16:36:48
- does ata ship pets 2006-03-01 17:10:35
- continental.com 2006-03-01 21:34:53
- pet shipping 2006-03-01 21:35:11
- broken bones in cat 2006-03-04 03:31:53
- cat has broken bones above base of tail vet said it will heal on its own 2006-03-04 03:32:53
- cat broken bones and diarreah 2006-03-04 03:58:24
- cat health 2006-03-04 14:10:22
- cat has broken bones wasn't bleeding before but now is and now she can't defecate too 2006-03-04 14:16:35
- mucous blood diarreah in cat 2006-03-04 14:22:47

It is not too difficult to understand what transpired through this three-day history of searches. The search engine data tells a story about a person and his or her cat.

This glut of user data raised a nearly endless number of questions and concerns. Primarily, it brought awareness to the fact that search engines know you better than you may like. Actually, they probably know you better than you know yourself in some ways. You tend to forget what you have searched for in the past; they don't. We may like to think that our searches are just quick queries, harmless and pointless inquiries known only to us. But the fact is that search engines keep all of that data, and most of them keep it forever. Google has recently begun to strip personal identifiers from the data after a certain time period has elapsed, but from the AOL searches we can see that this is sometimes still not enough.

Here is an AOL user whose searches tell a sad story (for sake of space, I have stripped out a large number of searches):

- body fat calliper 2006-03-01 18:54:10
- curb morning sickness 2006-03-05 08:53:23
- get fit while pregnant 2006-03-09 18:49:37
- he doesn't want the baby 2006-03-11 03:52:01
- uou're pregnant he doesn't want the baby 2006-03-11 03:52:49
- online christian colleges 2006-03-11 04:13:33
- foods to eat when pregnant 2006-03-12 09:38:02
- baby names and meanings 2006-03-14 20:01:27
- maternity clothes 2006-03-28 09:28:25
- pregnancy workout videos 2006-03-29 10:01:39
- what is yoga 2006-03-29 12:17:31
- what is theism 2006-03-29 12:18:30
- hindu religion 2006-03-29 12:18:56
- is yoga alligned with christianity 2006-03-29 12:33:18
- abortion clinics charlotte nc 2006-04-17 11:00:02
- can christians be forgiven for abortion 2006-04-17 21:14:19
- roe vs. wade 2006-04-17 22:22:07
- abortion clinic charlotte 2006-04-18 15:14:03
- symptoms of miscarriage 2006-04-18 16:14:07
- water aerobics charlotte nc 2006-04-18 19:41:27
- abortion clinic chsrlotte nc 2006-04-18 21:45:39
- engagement gifts 2006-04-20 16:57:04
- mom's turning 50 2006-04-20 17:51:13
- high risk abortions 2006-04-20 17:53:49
- abortion fibroid 2006-04-20 17:55:18
- wedding gown styles 2006-04-26 19:37:34
- recover after miscarriage 2006-05-22 18:17:53
- marry your live-in 2006-05-27 07:25:45

This woman goes from searching about pregnancy, to realizing that the father does not want to keep the baby, to researching abortion clinics, to researching whether she can, according to her faith, choose abortion. It seems that she did not have to face that decision, as the pregnancy terminated in a miscarriage. And at the end of it all, life goes on, and she seems ready to be married. We can reconstruct this period of her life by what she searched for. We know things about her that even her friends and her boyfriend would not know. Did he know that she was considering an abortion? Did he even know that she was pregnant? Did he know that she was wrestling with her faith? Her searches revealed her actions, her heart, her intentions. It was all there, sitting in a database at AOL. She had doubtlessly long forgotten about many of these searches; yet the search engine remembered.

What is remarkable about these searches is the way people transition seamlessly from the normal and mundane to the outrageous and perverse. In this way, the searches are an apt reflection of real life. The user who is in one moment searching for information about a computer game may in the next be looking for the most violent and degrading pornography imaginable. Back and forth it goes. One user went from searching for preteen pornography to searching for games appropriate for a church youth group. Others, spurned lovers, sought out ways of exacting revenge, while still others grappled with the moral implications of cheating on their spouses.

Our searches are a penetrating window into our hearts. We tell search engines what we would not tell anyone else; we ask them what we would be far too embarrassed to ask in any other context. And we entrust to them this information, perhaps not realizing that they might keep these searches forever and certainly trusting that they will never reveal it to anyone else. Though we may want them to forget about our searches, we now know that they do not.

More people than ever before are watching us, keeping tabs on us through our data. They are sorting through this data to find a picture of who we are. And someday they may make this data public. Our secrets may be revealed, if not today, at some later date. The challenge for the Christian is clear: we need to be diligent in living lives marked by what we believe. Christians must ensure that we are above reproach at all times—more guarded in our behavior, more diligent in our Christlikeness, than we've ever been. These words have always stirred me: "Now when they [members of the Jewish council] saw the boldness of Peter and John, and perceived that they were uneducated, common men, they were astonished. And they recognized that *they had been with Jesus*" (Acts 4:13, emphasis added). Wouldn't it be remarkable if the Numerati could see a distinct difference between the data trails Christians leave behind and the ones left behind by unbelievers—that our data trails made it obvious that we had been with Jesus? And wouldn't it be a shame if the data trails were nearly indistinguishable?

Ultimately, this visibility serves to remind us that we live all of our lives before the all-seeing eye of the Lord. "Nothing is hidden that will not be made manifest, nor is anything secret that will not be known and come to light" (Luke 8:17). While we live in the view of mobile phone carriers and Internet providers and search engines, we ultimately live before God, the One who sees all and knows all, and who will demand an accounting of every word, every deed, every moment we were given on this earth.

Seeing and Being Seen

In 2010, there were well over 4 billion photos on Flickr, and Facebook was reported to contain far more than that. Meanwhile YouTube is serving up tens of billions of videos every month. The vast majority of these photographs and videos are the product of amateurs rather than professionals. Some of the most popular YouTube videos are the most mundane. A dad driving his son home after a visit from the dentist has been seen over 65 million times ("David After Dentist"), and a little boy having his finger bitten by his baby brother has racked up well over 200 million views ("Charlie bit my finger—again!").

When something important happens, we are there, ready to capture one another as we deal with the situation. When nothing at all important happens, still we are there, capturing it and perhaps hoping that we will luck out and have it develop into something remarkable.

All of this visibility has grown into, or perhaps fostered, a love of seeing and being seen, on both an amateur and professional level. There is an irony here. On the one hand, we hate that we are always being seen. On the other hand, we love to be seen, to be noticed, to be made much of. The only thing worse than being seen is *not* being seen.

In early 2006, ABC was casting a new season of their smash-hit television show *Extreme Makeover: Home Edition*. The show had grown in popularity since its debut in 2004 and was now drawing almost 15 million viewers each week. In every episode, the cast and crew unexpectedly visits a family, one that has fallen on hard times or has seen a parent or child suffer from some illness. ABC sends the family on vacation; while the family is gone, their home is rebuilt. In March 2006, an ABC employee sent an e-mail to network affiliates asking them to help them find new families, new stories, for the show. She sent along a wish list of the kind of families they would like to find.

> We are open to any and ALL story ideas and are especially looking for the following:
>
> - Extraordinary Mom/Dad recently diagnosed with ALS
> - Family who has child with PROGERIA (aka "little old man disease")
> - Congenital insensitivity to pain with anhidrosis, referred to as CIPA by the few people who know about it. (There are 17 known cases in U.S.—let me know if one is in your town!) This is where kids cannot feel any physical pain.
> - Muscular Dystrophy Child—Amazing kid who is changing people's views about MD
> - MADD/Drunk Driving—Family turns tragedy into triumph after losing a child to drunk driving
> - Family who has multiple children w/ Down Syndrome (either adopted or biological)
> - Amazing/loved Mom or dad diagnosed w/ melanoma/skin cancer
> - Home Invasion—family robbed, house messed up (vandalized)— kids fear safety in their home now
> - Victims of hate crime in own home. Family's house victim of arson or severely vandalized

The network was looking for families that had been rocked by tragedy, seeking to turn this tragedy into our entertainment. After mentioning a disease that leaves people unable to feel pain, the writer of the e-mail chirps hopefully, "Let me know if one is in your town!"[4]

Extreme Makeover: Home Edition is just one of many shows that exploit people for the purpose of our entertainment, just one part of a wider phenomenon in our culture. We are a culture of exhibitionists, of people who behave in a way that attracts attention, people who are motivated by the desire to do things that will make people look at us. This feeds the ego or provides some kind of sick satisfaction. The popularity of shows like *Extreme Makeover: Home Edition* and *American Idol* is just one symptom of a greater disease manifesting itself in a strange fascination with parading ourselves in front of the world, allowing them to see us at our worst. Fifteen minutes of this kind of fame is somehow better than no fame at all.

YouTube is another symptom of this disease of exhibitionism, a place where all of us are free to post videos of ourselves that are often, by any measure, distasteful and embarrassing. We love to see people fail (epically!) and, for our own amusement, watch other people get injured.

We are exhibitionists, but we are also voyeurs, people who derive undue pleasure from observing others, from watching others in their worst moments or in their most private moments. This is the flip side of exhibitionism—the desire not just to be watched, but to watch, not just to be exploited, but to exploit. This is exactly what our culture promotes. Without our voyeuristic tendencies, our culture's obsession with exhibitionism would have no audience.

In reality television, YouTube, and countless other manifestations, exhibitionism and voyeurism have collided in a perfect storm of entertainment. We are drawn in by it and revel sometimes in the successes but more commonly in the failures of other people. We love to laugh at people who think they can sing when all evidence points to the opposite conclusion. We love to laugh along with the jabs and barbs that are sent their way and then to see them cry, swear, and storm off in shame and disgust. This passes for entertainment—and we love it. And much of it has grown out of our ability to see and be seen, to constantly show ourselves off to the rest of the world, and to persistently peer into the lives of others.

What happened to humility? What happened to respect? It seems that these qualities may have become a casualty of the digital era.

The Bible calls us to *humility*, going so far as to tell us that God will actively oppose those whose lives are marked by pride. Peter writes, "Clothe yourselves, all of you, with humility toward one another, for 'God opposes the proud but gives grace to the humble'" (1 Peter 5:5). Where is the humility in one who constantly desires to be seen, who craves the kind of attention that our digital technologies can so easily deliver? We do well to ask ourselves if we are living to please God, to receive his "well done, good and faithful servant" (Matthew 25:21), or whether we are living to receive the attention of others, to find a moment or two of joy in their short-lived enthusiasm. Are we happy with who and what God has made us to be, or are we seeking to be something else, especially to those who know about us only because of what we choose to reveal through our technology?

The Bible calls us to *respect*, telling us that respect is to be practiced by our pastors and elders and is to mark the relationship between husband and wife and between master and servant, reminding us that a wife's respect for her unbelieving husband can even be used by the Lord to lead him to faith. But where is the respect for one another when we mock those who experience tragedy, when their suffering becomes our entertainment? When we embrace the reality-show and YouTube forms of entertainment, we create a kind of lightness about life, with an emphasis not on what is weighty and eternal but on what is fleetingly entertaining. Our love for this type of entertainment spreads so that all of life becomes marked by disrespect, by lack of sobriety. We become what we love.

The Bible calls us to so much more. It calls us to live with discretion. The Bible calls us to live lives marked by humility, by respect for one another. It calls us to make little of ourselves so we can make much of Christ.

APPLICATION

Integrity and Security

When we look at the *theory* of technology, we see that great advances in technology tend to shift power, and sure enough, this has happened in the aftermath of the digital explosion. Each of us is, more than ever, living under the power of others.

Our Christian *theology* tells us that we cannot separate who we are from what we do—that our actions betray the state of our hearts. Therefore we are our digital detritus; the trails of data we leave behind us tell the stories of our lives, showing where we have been, what we have done, and who we truly are. They do not tell the whole story, but they certainly do tell part of it.

Our *experience* of life after the digital explosion tells us that we leave data behind us wherever we go and that this data can be used for us and against us. Sometimes this data is our friend; sometimes it is our foe. In either case, we are beginning to realize that we need to guard against the consequences of leaving too much of ourselves available to too many people. And yet we also see that there are ways in which we long to see and to be seen, ways in which we want to leave data behind for others to enjoy or to use in ways that benefit us.

Be aware. It is important that we remain aware that our digital devices leave trails behind them, just the way jets leave contrails in a cold sky. Search engines remember what we search for; cell phone companies remember where we have been; e-mail accounts remember what we've sent and received. In all the ways our devices give the pretense of allowing us to live private lives, they also expose us to the view of others. Our lives are lived in the public eye in unprecedented ways.

Develop character. In a culture that demands and is defined by entertainment, it can be difficult to emphasize character. And yet Christians need to be marked by godly character—by the humility and respect that seem so foreign to the entertainment we so love. Examine your entertainment, and examine your character. You may well find that there is a correlation between them, and that in order to grow in character, you will need to reform your entertainment, letting go of those things that are exhibitionist or exploitive and taking up those things that develop character rather than mar it.

Examine your trail. Though the trail you leave behind is not the complete story of your life, it is descriptive nonetheless. If you find that you are constantly worrying about what you are doing through your digital devices, if you are continually trying to clean up the trail you've left behind, it may be a good time to examine your motives. Are you concerned with privacy, or are you concerned with protecting yourself from the potential fallout of sinful decisions or addictions?

QUESTIONS FOR REFLECTION

1. Are there ways in which you like to see things that you know you should not see? Are there times you like to be seen?

2. What does your data trail say about you? Would you be willing for your spouse to see it? Your parents? Your pastors?

3. In what ways has your life changed by knowing that other people are always watching? Is this somehow different from knowing that God is always watching? Why or why not?

4. Can you see examples in your life in which your character has been shaped by exhibitionist or exploitive entertainment? What did you do about it? What will you do about it now?

The
NEXT STORY
and the
STORY AFTER THAT

I read a lot of books, and one thing that bothers me is when a book does not have a proper conclusion or, worse still, no conclusion at all. It just … ends. Too often, I read 200 pages, only to find that it leaves me hanging, failing to wrap things up and send me on my way. I do not want *The Next Story* to be that kind of book. Of course, books can also err in the other direction, using the conclusion as a place to drop in all of the arguments that somehow wouldn't fit anywhere else. I don't want to do that to you either.

I've said things in this book that are theoretical, theological, and, hopefully, practical. I hope I've given you a lot to think about along the way. I have deliberately tried to be more *descriptive* than *prescriptive*. I cannot tell you how you should live your life, and I certainly don't want to pretend that I know how to legislate the best way to live with technology in your home, with your family, at your job, or in your church. I want you to take what's true and have these things shape your relationship with technology in a way that suits your unique situation.

Maybe it will prove useful if I end on a personal note, telling you how I've changed in the process of writing of this book and, hopefully, in the living of this book. I began this book with a question, or a series of questions. I asked if technology was somehow taking over my life, if it was remaking me in its image, if it was making me a tool of my tools. I was dismayed but not surprised to find that in many ways this was exactly the case—except it wasn't so much that technology was taking over my life as I was just allowing it to push its way in. I was passive more than the fact that technology was active.

This book has been a long time in the writing—a year at least. And in that time, through all the research I've done, all the books I've read, I have made many changes to my perception of technology and my relationship with it. In other ways I've made changes and then reversed them, realizing that theory is difficult to turn into practice or that there are things I cannot change until those around me make the same shifts. If we all agreed that we would check our e-mail once a day, I could afford to be disciplined with it. But we expect people to e-mail throughout the day—my clients expect this, my friends, my fellow pastors. And so I feel like I need to go with the flow, checking e-mail multiple times rather than the one time I prefer to do.

So as I wrap up the book, let me share one big takeaway from each of those six areas in which we've seen great shifts in the aftermath of the digital explosion.

In chapter 4, we looked at living in a world of pervasive communication—a world in which communication has become one of the dominant paradigms through which we live our lives. I came to see that communication had become something of an idol in my life; there were ways in which I had raised it to a near-ultimate position. I felt out of the flow when I was not constantly checking e-mail, when I was disconnected and offline. But even more, I came to see the great privilege and responsibility that come with these amazing new means of communication. I saw ways in which I am prone to use them poorly, in which I do not use them to speak truth in love. This was a good heart check for me, a time to renew my sense of responsibility to use them for God's glory. And so I made course corrections. I've sought to emphasize encouragement through my words. I've sought to do a lot less writing about things that are wrong in the church or wrong in my life so I could focus instead on the many blessings God has bestowed on me. Overall, I've sought to discipline myself not just in how much I say but in the things I say through these great new media.

Chapter 5 was an examination of the role of mediation in our lives. As I studied mediation, I quickly came to see that I was prone to rely on more-mediated communication in times when it would be far better to use less-mediated. I had developed a kind of comfort with mediation so that I would often rather send an e-mail than pick up the phone. I was growing intimidated by face-to-face contact and in some ways was diminishing in my ability to do it well. In this way I would unintentionally alienate people; I would give less of me to them when they really needed more. So I made a change in course, attempting to rely less on the worse forms of communication. While I still send plenty of e-mails, I try to emphasize the importance of face-to-face contact, understanding that every e-mail sent comes at the expense of time spent looking into another person's eyes. I spend more time with people now, meeting them, being with them. When this is not possible, I am trying to phone instead of e-mail or video chat instead of phone.

Distraction was the topic of chapter 6. I have always been easily distracted and prone to let my mind wander. As I looked at digital distraction, I saw that this has been particularly challenging. And this was the most difficult of all the changes I had to make, one in which there were many course corrections. I came to realize that I like distraction and at times even crave it. Each distraction brings with it a bit of hope, a bit of joy. Would this e-mail be the *really* important one? Would this Facebook update give me something to laugh at? And yet amid all of the distraction, I found that I could accomplish little. I spent so much time being distracted that my work was disjointed and incomplete. In the end all I could do was find certain times in which I would have to ensure that I was focusing on just one thing. I found programs that would block websites during certain hours and learned to shut down every program but the one I was using. I learned to leave my devices in my office after-hours so I could focus on my family without the distractions of beeps and buzzes. This has probably been the biggest change—coming to see that if I was going to be truly present with the people I love, I had to stop being drawn away by the cell phone, the laptop, and all the other devices that continue to scream for my attention.

In chapter 7 we turned to the issue of information and informationism. And once again, I saw that I had succumbed to its allure. I had neglected to be diligent in focusing on knowledge and wisdom ahead of data and information. I came to understand that I was drowning in a sea of information and that the sheer volume of information I was encountering actually prohibited me from growing in knowledge and wisdom. The thing that I loved was choking me. And so very quickly I sought to reduce inputs and to spend more time encountering the best information and less time encountering the least significant. I unsubscribed from lots of blogs, even many that I truly enjoyed, because I was not benefiting from their information; I tried to de-emphasize e-mail so that I received fewer of them;

I even canceled delivery of the newspaper. And slowly I felt my head begin to clear as I spent more time thinking about fewer things.

Chapter 8 examined truth and authority, and I spent a lot of time discussing search engines and Wikipedia. I had always regarded the wiki model with some suspicion. Having done the research and scrutinized the model more thoroughly, my suspicion grew. Though I still use Wikipedia, I use it largely to do basic research related to issues that are just not very important (which I think is quite an indictment of it). The more important the issue, the less likely I am to use Wikipedia. I've also had to consider the nature of truth to ensure that I am not allowing the consensus or relevance models of truth to change how I perceive what is true. The biggest change here has been a return to the past—not necessarily to the sources of information from the past, but to the model of knowing truth. In response to truth coming by consensus, truth being crowdsourced, I tend to look for more and better authority.

And chapter 9 dealt with visibility and privacy, with issues related to Big Brother and Little Brother. The first realization here was our love of seeing and being seen, and quickly I found myself disgusted rather than intrigued by so many of the videos and websites that share funny and embarrassing moments. I found that laughing at other people's pain and failure just isn't that funny. Meanwhile, when I came to understand data trails, how I constantly leave these trails behind me, I became much more aware of what I was leaving behind me and what it might mean. I came to see the wisdom in being mindful here, understanding that what I do will live on somewhere on the Internet. Knowing that what I say now may be used against me twenty years from now taught me that I need to guard every word, that I need to be aware of everything I do and see.

I wrote my first book in 2007 and realized as I typed out its final words that if I was going to be so bold as to put it into print, if I was going to ask people to trust me, to read the words I had written, that I needed to live them first. I could not suggest how others ought to live and what they should believe until I had already sought to do these things to the best of my abilities. And in this way I've tried to live *The Next Story*. I can attest that there is freedom from the challenges that come in this strange new world. The challenges will remain; there will always be new ones. But when we know what is true, when we know what is true about our hearts and true about technology, we can be prepared to respond with wisdom and discernment so that we can live with true virtue in this, the aftermath of the digital explosion. We *can* live in a God-honoring way in the next story, and in the story after that as well.

ACKNOWLEDGMENTS

Writing acknowledgments at the end of a book may seem like an odd tradition, and perhaps in many ways it is. But when you've been through the months of work that go into writing a book like this one, you do learn gratitude and do want to express it. These few words are one way of doing this.

To that end …

Thanks to all the people who have made my blog a part of their lives. It is truly humbling that you've chosen to do so, and it is my prayer that I'll find ways of serving you well through that rather unexpected ministry. I appreciate your prayers, support, love, and page views.

Thanks to the people at Wolgemuth & Associates (Andrew, mostly) and the people at Zondervan (Ryan, Chris, and others) who dreamed up this book with me and who played pivotal roles in bringing it to life.

Thanks to Travis and Chris for keeping my website running while I was way too busy and/or ignorant to do so, and to David Kjos for all of your quiet but consistent behind-the-scenes work at the blog. Thanks to David Murray for being a good friend, podcast cohost, and a guy who is willing to hear (and share) ideas related to this topic and so much else.

Thanks to the men, women, and children of Grace Fellowship Church. There was a rare Sunday in the writing of this book when fewer than ten people asked me, "How is the book going?" Your constant prayers made all the difference, I'm convinced. Thanks for letting the Challies be a part of this church family. You are a great blessing to us.

Thanks to my fellow elders, Julian, Paul, and Murray. I am thrilled to be able to serve alongside such godly brothers. You guys are one of the highlights of every week.

Thanks to my family—moms and dads, siblings and siblings-in-law, nieces, nephews, and assorted others who defy easy labeling (you know who you are).

Nick, Abby, and Michaela, thanks for your patience, your prayers, and your love. I know that Daddy owes you an August after disappearing for most of the last one. I'll make it up to you guys. Thanks to Nick for taking an interest in the book; Abby for making me pictures to brighten my day; Michaela for being deliberate about learning to sleep through the night so Daddy wouldn't be too tired to write the next day. You guys are awesome, and I'm proud to be your dad.

And thanks to Aileen, without whom this book (and its author) would be a complete mess. Words fail as I try to pen a few that might express your impact and importance in the writing of this book. And they fail as I seek to express my love for you. It is an honor to be married to you, and I thank God for giving me such a precious gift.

NOTES

Preface

1. "*Big Ivan*, The Tsar Bomba ('King of Bombs')," *Nuclear Weapon Archive*: nuclearweaponarchive.org/Russia/TsarBomba.html (June 1, 2010).

2. Viktor Adamsky and Yuri Smirnov, "Moscow's Biggest Bomb: The 50-Megaton Test of October 1961," *Cold War International History Project* 4 (Fall 1994): 3.

Introduction :: The Digital Explosion

1. Thanks to Danny Hillis for granting permission to quote his poem.

2. Steve Maich, "Malcolm Gladwell," *Canadian Business* 83 (March 16, 2010): 58. You have read some of Gladwell's books, haven't you? If not, you are impoverishing yourself. Start with *The Tipping Point* and then go to *Blink* and *Outliers*. If you prefer shorter reading, buy *What the Dog Saw*, his series of greatest hits from *The New Yorker*. It is good, but not quite as good as the others.

3. Thanks to my friend David Murray for this skillfully alliterated breakdown.

Chapter 1 :: Discerning Technology

1. Nancy Pearcey, *Total Truth* (Wheaton, Ill.: Crossway, 2004), 47.

2. Adapted from Stephen V. Monsma, ed., *Responsible Technology* (Grand Rapids: Eerdmans, 1986), 19. Thanks to John Dyer for working with me on this definition.

3. Albert Borgmann, *Power Failure* (Grand Rapids: Brazos, 2003), 8.

4. Neil Postman, "Five Things We Need to Know About Technological Change," *UPM*: www.mat.upm.es/~jcm/neil-postman--five-things.html (July 10, 2010).

5. Ibid.

6. Timothy Keller, *Counterfeit Gods* (New York: Dutton, 2009), xvi.

7. Ibid., xvii.

8. Mihail C. Roco and William Sims Bainbridge, eds., *Converging Technologies for Improving Human Performance* (Dordrecht: Kluwer, 2002), 293.

Chapter 2 :: Understanding Technology

1. Neil Postman, "Five Things We Need to Know About Technological Change," *UPM*: www.mat.upm.es/~jcm/neil-postman--five-things.html (July 10, 2010). Most of these are drawn from Postman's lecture. Despite the dry title it is a brilliant lecture. Though slightly dated in some ways, it remains well worth reading.

2. Postman, "Five Things We Need to Know."

3. Mark Federman, "What Is the Meaning of The Medium is the Message?" (July 23, 2004). Retrieved November 18, 2010, from http://individual.utoronto.ca/markfederman/article_mediumisthemessage.htm.

4. Ibid.

5. Marshall McLuhan, *Understanding Media* (New York: McGraw Hill, 1964), 199.

6. Postman, "Five Things We Need to Know."

7. Ibid.

8. See Marshall McLuhan and Eric McLuhan, *Laws of Media* (Toronto: University of Toronto Press, 1988), 7.

9. Postman, "Five Things We Need to Know" (his second idea).

10. See Don Tapscott, *Grown Up Digital* (New York: McGraw Hill, 2009), 100.

11. See Gary Small and Gigi Vorgan, *iBrain* (New York: HarperCollins, 2008), 18.

12. The book *Wired for Intimacy* by William M. Struthers (Downers Grove, Ill.: InterVarsity, 2009) offers a compelling look at this.

Chapter 3 :: A Digital History

1. Stephen E. Ambrose, *Undaunted Courage* (New York: Simon & Schuster, 1996), 52.

2. Tom Standage, *The Victorian Internet* (New York: Walker, 1998).

3. See Neil Postman, *Technopoly* (New York: Vintage, 1993), 67.

4. Neil Postman, *Amusing Ourselves to Death* (New York: Viking, 1985), 67.

5. Ibid.

6. Ibid., 69.

7. John P. Robinson, "I Love My TV," *American Demographics* (September 1990), 24.

8. Council for Research Excellence, "Video Consumer Mapping Study" (Ball State University's Center for Media Design, March 26, 2009), www.researchexcellence.com/vcmstudy.php.

9. See Shane Hipps, *Flickering Pixels* (Grand Rapids: Zondervan, 2009), 76–77.

10. Ibid., 78.

11. See John Palfrey and Urs Gasser, *Born Digital* (New York: Basic, 2008). I rely on this book for much of the information in these next two sections.

12. U.S. Census Bureau, "Home Computers and Internet Use in the United States: August 2000" (September 2001). View the report at www.census.gov/prod/2001pubs/p23-207.pdf.

13. "Industry Facts," *The Entertainment Software Association*: www.theesa.com/facts/index.asp.

Chapter 4 :: Speaking, Truthing, Loving, Living

1. To learn about Newton, I recommend starting with Jonathan Aitken's biographical work *John Newton: From Disgrace to Amazing Grace* (Wheaton, Ill.: Crossway, 2007).

2. Os Guinness, *The Call: Finding and Fulfilling the Central Purpose of Your Life* (Nashville: Nelson, 2003), 88.

3. David Van Biema, "The New Calvinism," *Time*: www.time.com/time/specials/packages/article/0,28804,1884779_1884782_1884760,00.html (August 1, 2010).

4. See Jon Agar, *Constant Touch* (London: Icon, 2003), 3–5.

5. "The Social Media Habits of Women 18–34," *Radio Business Report*: www.rbr.com/media-news/research/25649.html (August 1, 2010).

6. Amanda Lenhart, Kristen Purcell, Aaron Smith, and Kathryn Zickuhr, "Social Media and Mobile Internet Use Among Teens and Young Adults," *Pew Research Center Publications*: http://pewresearch.org/pubs/1484/social-media-mobile-internet-use-teens-millennials-fewer-blog (August 2, 2010).

7. April Frawley Birdwell, "Addicted to Phones?" *The Post*: newsletter for the University of Florida Health Science Center: http://news.health.ufl.edu/media/2010/01/ThePost_Feb07.pdf (August 2, 2010).

8. Bruce Waltke, *The Book of Proverbs: Chapters 15–31* (Grand Rapids: Eerdmans, 2005), 86.

9. Charles Bridges, *Proverbs* (Wheaton, Ill.: Crossway, 2001), 159.

10. Ibid.

11. Derek Kidner, *Proverbs* (Downers Grove, Ill.: InterVarsity, 2009), 46.

12. See R. Albert Mohler Jr., *He Is Not Silent* (Chicago: Moody, 2008), 42.

13. John Stott, *The Message of Ephesians* (Downers Grove, Ill.: InterVarsity, 1979), 172.

14. Frederick M. Lehman, "The Love of God" (Kansas City: Nazarene, 1917, 1945).

Chapter 5 :: Life in the Real World

1. Todd Gitlin, *Media Unlimited* (New York: Holt, 2007), 20.

2. Council for Research Excellence, "Video Consumer Mapping Study" (Ball State University's Center for Media Design, March 26, 2009), www.researchexcellence.com/vcmstudy.php.

3. R. C. Sproul, *The Holiness of God* (Carol Stream, Ill.: Tyndale House, 2000), 22.

4. Douglas Groothuis, *The Soul in Cyberspace* (Grand Rapids: Baker, 1997), 38.

5. Ibid., 39.

6. John Freeman, *The Tyranny of E-mail: The Four-Thousand-Year Journey to Your Inbox* (New York: Simon and Schuster, 2009), 106–7.

7. Rebecca Winters Keegan, "Q&A with James Cameron," *Time*: www.time.com/time/arts/article/0,8599,1576622,00.html (July 9, 2010).

8. Groothuis, *Soul in Cyberspace*, 40.

9. Ibid., 47.

10. Ibid., 26.

11. Barry Wellman et al., "The Social Affordances of the Internet for Networked Individualism," *Journal of Computer-Mediated Communication*, http://jcmc.indiana.edu/vol8/issue3/wellman.html (June 20, 2010).

12. Ibid.

13. Douglas Estes, *SimChurch* (Grand Rapids: Zondervan, 2009), 18.

14. Ibid., 26.

15. Philip Edgcumbe Hughes, *A Commentary on the Epistle to the Hebrews* (Grand Rapids: Eerdmans, 1977), 415.

16. Ibid.

17. Charles D. Drew, *A Journey Worth Taking: Finding Your Purpose in This World* (Phillipsburg, N.J.: P & R, 2007).

18. Ian Shapira, "Texting Generation Doesn't Share Boomers' Taste for Talk," *The Washington Post*: www.washingtonpost.com/wp-dyn/content/article/2010/08/07/AR2010080702848.html (July 5, 2010).

19. Quoted in ibid.

Chapter 6 :: Turn Off and Tune In

1. See Virginia Heffernan, "Beep!" *The New York Times*: www.nytimes.com/2010/03/21/magazine/21FOB-medium-t.htm?_r=1 (August 25, 2010).

2. Paul Graham, "Disconnecting Distraction," http://paulgraham.com/distraction.html (May 3, 2010).

3. Jarice Hanson, *24/7: How Cell Phones and the Internet Change the Way We Live, Work, and Play* (Westport, Conn.: Praeger, 2007), 9.

4. See Edward T. Hall, *The Dance of Life* (Garden City, N.Y.: Anchor, 1984).

5. Hanson, *24/7*, 10.

6. "Global Survey Shows Cell Phone Is 'Remote Control' for Life," *Synovate*: www.synovate.com/news/article/2009/09/global-survey-shows-cell-phone-is-remote-control-for-life-42-of-americans-can-t-live-without-it-and-almost-half-sleep-with-it-nearby.html (May 31, 2010).

7. Matt Richtel, "The Lure of Data: Is It Addictive?" *The New York Times*: www.nytimes.com/2003/07/06/business/the-lure-of-data-is-it-addictive.html (August 1, 2010).

8. Gary Small and Gigi Vorgan, *iBrain* (New York: HarperCollins, 2008), 18.

9. See "Interview: Clifford Nass," *Frontline: Growing Up Online: digital_nation*: www.pbs.org/wgbh/pages/frontline/digitalnation/interviews/nass.html.

10. Helen Walters, "Google's Irene Au: On Design Challenges," *BusinessWeek*: www.businessweek.com/innovate/content/mar2009/id20090318_786470.htm; see discussion in Nicholas Carr, *The Shallows* (New York: Norton, 2010), 156–57.

11. Carr, *The Shallows*, 157.

12. Ibid., 138.

13. This seems like the logical place to add a plug for my book *The Discipline of Spiritual Discernment* (Wheaton, Ill.: Crossway, 2007). It examines this topic in much greater detail.

14. Thanks to Joel Hilliker and his article "How to Think Deeply" for inspiring much of this section (*The Trumpet*: www.thetrumpet.com/index.php?q=1060.366.63.0 [June 6, 2010]).

Aside :: Your Family and Media

1. These are drawn from David Murray's DVD series titled *God's Technology*. For more information, visit www.HeadHeartHand.org.

Chapter 7 :: More Is Better

1. Quoted in Alorie Gilbert, "Why Can't You Pay Attention Anymore?" *CNET News*: http://news.cnet.com/Why-cant-you-pay-attention-anymore/2008-1022_3-5637632.html (July 31, 2010).

2. "Data, Information, Knowledge, and Wisdom," *University of Oregon: Oregon Technology in Education Council*: http://otec.uoregon.edu/data-wisdom.htm (August 1, 2010).

3. T. S. Eliot, "The Rock" (1934).

4. Nicholas Carr, *The Shallows* (New York: Norton, 2010), 133.

5. See Clay Shirky, "It's Not Information Overload. It's Filter Failure," *Blip.tv*: http://web2expo.blip.tv/file/1277460/ (August 6, 2010).

6. See John Gantz and David Reinsel, "The Digital Universe Decade—Are You Ready?" (May 2010) *IDIC iView*: http://idcdocserv.com/925 (December 1, 2010).

7. Quentin Schultze, *Habits of the High-Tech Heart* (Grand Rapids: Baker, 2002), 26.

8. Torkel Klingberg, *The Overflowing Brain* (Oxford: Oxford University Press, 2009), 103.

9. Ibid., 165.

10. John Naish, *Enough: Breaking Free from the World of More* (London: Hodder & Stoughton, 2008), 28.

11. Klingberg, *Overflowing Brain*, 7.

12. Douglas Adams, *The Hitchhiker's Guide to the Galaxy: A Trilogy in Four Parts* (London: Pan, 1992), 178.

13. Schultze, *Habits of the High-Tech Heart*, 32.

14. Ibid., 33.

15. See Carr, *The Shallows*, 180.

16. Ibid.

17. Ibid., 191.

18. See Viktor Mayer-Schönberger, *Delete* (Princeton: Princeton University Press, 2009), 2.

19. Ibid., 3.

Chapter 8 :: Here Comes Everybody

1. George Johnson, "The Nitpicking of the Masses vs. the Authority of the Experts," *The New York Times*: www.nytimes.com/2006/01/03/science/03comm.html (August 25, 2010).

2. Wayne Grudem, *Systematic Theology* (Grand Rapids: Zondervan, 2000), 195.

3. Ibid., 196.

4. Ibid.

5. "Wikipedia:About," *Wikipedia*: http://en.wikipedia.org/wiki/Wikipedia:About.

6. "The Word—Wikiality," *The Colbert Report*: www.colbertnation.com/the-colbert-report-videos/72347/july-31-2006/the-word---wikiality.

7. Oliver Kamm, "Knowledge by Consensus," *The First Post*: www.thefirstpost.co.uk/46900,news-comment,news-politics,knowledge-by-consensus-wikipedia-jimmy-wales (July 2, 1010).

8. "Wikipedia: 'A Work in Progress,'" *BusinessWeek*: www.businessweek.com/technology/content/dec2005/tc20051214_441708.htm (December 1, 2010).

9. Thanks to Ryan of www.striderseo.com for assistance in helping me understand how Google measures relevance.

10. H. D. McDonald, "Authority," in *Zondervan Encyclopedia of the Bible*, rev. ed., Merrill C. Tenney, ed. (Grand Rapids: Zondervan, 2009), 1:451.

11. Andrew Keen, *The Cult of the Amateur* (New York: Doubleday, 2007).

12. James Doran, "Wikipedia Chief Promises Change After 'Expert' Exposed as Fraud," *Times Online*: http://technology.timesonline.co.uk/tol/news/tech_and_web/article1480012.ece (August 26, 2010).

13. See Keen, *Cult of the Amateur*, 68–69.

Chapter 9 :: Seeing and Being Seen

1. Stephen Baker, *The Numerati* (New York: Houghton Mifflin, 2008), 9.

2. Ibid.

3. Ibid., 7.

4. "ABC's 'Extreme Exploitation,'" The Smoking Gun: www.thesmokinggun.com/file/abcs-extreme-exploitation (December 1, 2010).

Share Your Thoughts

With the Author: Your comments will be forwarded to
the author when you send them to *zauthor@zondervan.com*.

With Zondervan: Submit your review of this book
by writing to *zreview@zondervan.com*.

Free Online Resources at
www.zondervan.com

Zondervan AuthorTracker: Be notified whenever your favorite
authors publish new books, go on tour, or post an update
about what's happening in their lives at www.zondervan.com/
authortracker.

Daily Bible Verses and Devotions: Enrich your life with daily
Bible verses or devotions that help you start every morning
focused on God. Visit www.zondervan.com/newsletters.

Free Email Publications: Sign up for newsletters on Christian
living, academic resources, church ministry, fiction, children's
resources, and more. Visit www.zondervan.com/newsletters.

Zondervan Bible Search: Find and compare Bible passages in
a variety of translations at www.zondervanbiblesearch.com.

Other Benefits: Register yourself to receive online benefits
like coupons and special offers, or to participate in research.

ZONDERVAN

ZONDERVAN.com/
AUTHORTRACKER
follow your favorite authors